ABOUT THE COVER ILLUSTRATION

What happens when trees grown up tall and slender in a forest environment must adapt to an open grassland and cattle grazing at their roots? They get the shakes--ring shakes.

I sketched this tree after viewing black walnut trees that had been left on their own following clearing of a forest for pasture. My sketch does not show the awe-inspiring height of these trees caused by competition for sunlight within a community of trees.

The sadness is these valuable forest trees rarely survive this habitat change. Strong winds stretch the wood fibers holding the tree together. Breaks that develop between their rings invite infection, causing the decline and death of these would-be monarchs.

FEMALE FORESTER

FOREVER

Charlotte Schneider

BALBOA.
PRESS
A DIVISION OF HAY HOUSE

Balboa Press books may be ordered through booksellers or by contacting:

Balboa Press
A Division of Hay House
1663 Liberty Drive
Bloomington, IN 47403
www.balboapress.com
1-(877) 407-4847

Because of the dynamic nature of the Internet, any web addresses or links contained in this book may have changed since publication and may no longer be valid. The views expressed in this work are solely those of the author and do not necessarily reflect the views of the publisher, and the publisher hereby disclaims any responsibility for them.

The author of this book does not dispense medical advice or prescribe the use of any technique as a form of treatment for physical, emotional, or medical problems without the advice of a physician, either directly or indirectly. The intent of the author is only to offer information of a general nature to help you in your quest for emotional and spiritual well-being. In the event you use any of the information in this book for yourself, which is your constitutional right, the author and the publisher assume no responsibility for your actions.

Any people depicted in stock imagery provided by Thinkstock are models, and such images are being used for illustrative purposes only.
Certain stock imagery © Thinkstock.

Printed in the United States of America

ISBN: 978-1-4525-6550-7 (sc)
ISBN: 978-1-4525-6551-4 (e)
ISBN: 978-1-4525-6552-1 (hc)

Library of Congress Control Number: 2012923591

Balboa Press rev. date: 03/26/2013

Sometimes when you are breaking new ground
it is better to be a weed than a tree.
C. E. SCHNEIDER, 2002

TABLE OF CONTENTS

FOREWORD

Upon entering Charlotte's home she has a big poster that shows hands cupped together holding soil along with a small pine tree.

The caption reads.

**What we are is God's gift to us
Who we become is our gift to God.**

Eleanor Powell

Charlotte has been gifted with a passion for trees, the forest, and above all God. Her story tells of how being in the right place, at the right time, enabled her to pursue a career that had more to do with timing and divine intercession than with knowing what she wanted to do with the rest of her life.

Having been a secretary for over 10 years she joined the Sierra Club to have fun and to learn about backpacking. That choice took her in a new direction which gave her the opportunity to tap into and experience a joy that she had known as a child. A child who did not receive satisfaction from playing with dolls but the child who needed to be coaxed out of a tree because she had to wash up and help with dinner. A path was laid out early on, hidden under all the things that grown-ups somehow, simply forgot, or chose to ignore.

The time was early 70's when the Affirmative Action Law was mandated, allowing women to compete for jobs that had been exclusively male positions. Prior to those early days even if you wanted to have an education in a field such as forestry it was unavailable, because the colleges did not have the facilities to accommodate women with the required curriculum.

Although Charlotte's passion for knowledge and understanding of trees blinded her to the harsh realities that she would encounter in her new chosen field, she did roll up her sleeves and worked twice as hard with the hope of being recognized for her talents. In those early days being female was not a blessing or was it? Maybe not in her career in forestry as forestry was only a limb of her journey. Her journey would include a deeper intimate relationship with God. Her journey also included MS.

With lemons we are all supposed to make lemonade. Today Charlotte is still fighting, as hard, if not harder then she did in those early days. Her journey continues on a new and different path. A path fueled by disciplines learned from past experiences.

With MS they say there is no cure. In her doctor's office, on the wall, a message for all his patients, inscribed in large letters: **God made the body to be self-healing; whether you think you can or you think you can't you're right!** Charlotte believes in faith, hope and the love of God. She also believes in hard work, prayer and discipline.

If you find fear holding you back from realizing your dreams, you may be inspired by her story and like Charlotte keep pushing forward **one day at a time**.

Renee Quackenbush

PART 1

Forestry

CHAPTER 1

Adventure In The Mysterious Forest

I WAS WORKING FOR THE STATE forestry department cruising timber for a Missouri landowner. I sampled and measured the trees in plots in a grid pattern on this somewhat large (>100 acres) tract of timber, called cruising. The plots help to determine quantity and health of the timber as well as other resources like wildlife benefits to make recommendations for improvement.

It was a pleasant day in early summer in Washington County. Large-columned clouds moved briskly across the sky. I had been cruising timber for several hours, and as I crested the ridge I spotted a dark and ominous accumulation of clouds moving in my direction. My cruise and sample plots were nearly complete so I pushed on cruising toward the narrow valley that would provide exit from the area, knowing full well the storm would catch me.

Sure enough the rain started just as I finished my last plot. Knowing my vehicle was a couple miles away across country on the other side of a large creek was not real encouraging. The vehicle was probably safe, but I wondered about wadding across the wide and open creek and gambled on my probable safety. There is a certain lag time between when the rain hits the hillside and when it ultimately spills into the floodplain, and I gambled this storm would be hard and fast but not long and lingering.

The rain fell hard, like standing under a waterfall. I could not see very far ahead, perhaps about 30 feet. The slope became very steep as I descended to the valley. Wet sticks on the forest floor are as predictable as an oil-slick road in a light rain. A girl could find herself landing unceremoniously on a bed of wet leaves. Bad as that was the lightning was intense. If I knew then what I know now about lightning and the precarious position I was in, I would have fallen to my knees and prayed. Ignorance and stupidity go hand in hand.

I made it to the narrow valley between two ridges. There a small creek was tumbling and rushing to empty into the large valley where my vehicle was waiting. The creek did not look threatening, it was just a summer thunderstorm, so I took refuge under a rock outcrop next to a large tree stump. Had I considered that the old tree with the protective 3' wide, 6' tall stump had probably been blown apart by lightning some decades ago, I might have changed my mind. No, probably not.

The storm was raging, with violent flashes of lightning and ear-splitting thunder. Summer thunderstorms are fierce but typically of short duration, so I just enjoyed the show. The lightning lit up the valley like some crazy out-of-synch strobe lights. Thunder crashed and growled. The dead tree stump protected me from the sideways slant of the rain. The beauty of this valley and forest in the throes of this violent summer storm was overwhelming.

While I watched the storm flash and rock the narrow valley a poem was forming in my mind. St. Francis of Assisi also came to mind. I don't know why, I hadn't thought of him in years. I felt really peaceful as I waited out the storm. The poem seemed like a gift inspired by St. Francis. I included the poem at the end of this section.

The storm slowed and I emerged from under the rock ledge beside the tree stump. I followed the noisy stream down the narrow valley in the direction of the large creek bed. My boots splashed on the wet, rocky ground. The rain-swelled stream tumbled along the rocks in the narrow valley keeping me company. Patches of sunlight began to show through the trees tops far overhead. Then I stepped out of the woods into the wide valley where the small stream rushed into the creek bed, its load of water quickly lost in the wide gravel bar. As I sloshed across the creek to the vehicle, only slightly deeper at this time, the sun shone warmly on me, pulling the water from my wet clothes. My boots were hopelessly soaked.

Though somewhat remarkable for the grand show nature presented, it really was just another spectacular day in the life of a forester.

Rain

I love you rain,
for you are my life.
Your gentle touch plants flowers at my feet.
You plait my hair with scented vines.
Your waters cleanse my limbs
And wash the hurt from my soul.

I fear you rain,
for you are my death.
Your mother's sharp tongue tears me
limb from limb;
Your father's thundering voice shakes
my foundations.
You make the waters rise and tear the ground
from beneath my feet.

I need you, Rain, for I am your tree.

CHARLOTTE E. SCHNEIDER

CHAPTER 2

Embracing University Life

*A mind once stretched by a new idea can never
go back to its original dimension.*
OLIVER WENDELL HOLMES

*The greatest pleasure in life is in doing what
other people say you cannot do.*
WALTER BAGEHOT

YOUNG AND OLD, WITH DIFFERENT backgrounds, education, dreams, religions, races, and ethnic backgrounds, from every country, come together in a university. Surrounded by opportunities for learning, it is habit forming; the hunger can be insatiable. Education unlocked doors…doors I did not even know existed.

Though nothing compared to current costs, college was expensive. I came in with some savings, but not nearly enough. But my secretarial experience got me a work study position in the wood science research laboratory, where they studied the cell structure of the tree and how it reacts to change. The research reports available there from a variety of universities were fascinating! After ten years as a secretary, I finally knew what I wanted to be when I grew up--a forester. In August 1974, 10 years after high school graduation, I moved to Columbia Missouri and registered for my first semester of Forest Management. The science curriculum required two years of science classes such as physics and chemistry. I was never much on math in high school, but I sure learned it in college...in chemistry. Word problems used to drive me nuts as a child! In chemistry I learned I could logically solve very complicated problems. Twelve inches equals one foot never meant so much to me. I found once you get all the conversions laid out, any(?) problem is easy, you just multiply and divide. Wow!

There is one thing I never learned in college: a simple, easy, sure-fire way to study. I would study for days before an exam as if my life depended on the exam. Yet in the exam I would often get cold sweats. My mind would race out of control. It was awful! I must have done something right, because I graduated *cum laude*, barely, with a 3.001. It is amazing. I am not what you would consider intelligent. I used the old tried and true technique: repeat, repeat, repeat. It may be old fashioned, but it worked, enough to get me into *Xi Sigma Pi* (the honorary forestry fraternity) in 1976. I even had a semester as vice president. I had a passion for forestry which knew no bounds. I cannot say school was fun, it had its moments, but that piece of paper, that gradation certificate, was wonderful! I became addicted to information and forestry research.

The work study job didn't pay that much, but it was enough. Savings, working at the school, and a summer fighting fires in California paid the bills. Of course, I sold my car and bought a bicycle. It helped that I came in with a semester's worth of hours at night school from a local St. Louis community college. Little did I know I would be back there twenty years later catching up on horticulture. My parents must have helped, but if they had known the costs they would have had heart failure. I was pretty independent; they probably were wondering what I was doing studying forestry.

Another summer I attended forestry summer camp in the woods of Southern Missouri. It was hot! Streams of sweat were running down my back while the teacher lectured about natural pine regeneration. [The wind can blow pine seeds over an area where vegetation is lost due to harvest, fire, or storms. In time a new forest appears through the brushy vegetation.] The poison ivy I had at summer camp, swelling my eyes shut and blistering my neck and arms, added to my experience. And there were ticks sucking my blood. But learning about the forest made it all worthwhile. And forest surveying taught me a crew could survey through thick brush most any strange geometric shape and still come out at, or near, the point of beginning.

Classes like dendrology, measurements, geology, and silviculture forged the link that tied me to the forest. I learned to walk through the woods calling the trees by name. Forestry was fascinating. Trees were measured as an economic commodity, but needed to be understood as a biological organism. Trees are living, breathing plants which are cut down to make houses, furniture, books, artwork, wooden spoons, gunstocks, baskets, picture frames, and pallets that carry enormous sophisticated equipment. The spirit of the tree can live well beyond its natural life.

In my spare time, in preparation for a forestry conclave competition, I learned how to work a two-man bucksaw with a friend and fellow student. Whew! I don't know how the pioneers did it. I watched a young fellow practicing for the competition on log chopping. With a true aim and a lot of solid muscles, and a sharp ax, the chips flew while he cut through the log. And that is the way log cabins were built.

Personally, I don't know that I ever understood the full impact of what I was doing studying forest management. Classmates were mostly all male. Their being ten years younger than me probably helped me keep my concentration (?). I didn't think much about the future; I lived from one test to the next, one week to the next, one semester to the next. I studied and worked and studied. Just about the time I was thinking the semester would never, ever end, I was signing up for the next semester and piling new books into my bag.

Dressing up and Friday night happy hours at a local bistro just didn't happen; I didn't have time or money for such frivolity. A beer at the local pub was a rare event. Was the change worth it? Absolutely! Since then I have spent much time alone in the woods, but I never felt alone. Despite being miles from civilization, I felt very much at home among the trees, except for the ticks, chiggers, gnats and myriad of other insects. It was a job others only dream of. It was unbelievably grand. I felt, and saw, and smelled and dreamed. I thank God for my memories. Thank you School of Forestry for preparing me for this adventure.

Truthfully, I do remember a celebration where, after imbibing a few beers, friends and I wandered down to the columns for a solstice wolf howl at midnight. The university police came and, deciding we were harmless, suggested we quit; we were scaring some students studying late in a nearby tower. Some of us really knew how to howl; the time I had spent at the Wolf Sanctuary in St. Louis and with friends and their wolves certainly qualified me.

> *"…I shall be telling this with a sigh*
> *Somewhere ages and ages hence*
> *Two roads diverged in a wood, and I-*
> *1 took the one less traveled by,*
> *And that has made all the difference."*
> ROBERT FROST, "The Road Not Taken"

CHAPTER 3

The Forest Seasons

A S A CAREER, FORESTRY WAS very disappointing. But as a daily job, it was wonderful! I highly recommend the challenge and adventure. Consider first where I came from. As a secretary, working inside, when a storm came employees gathered at the windows to watch. Now I was in the storm, a part of the glory. The smell of the woods changes dramatically after a storm. The air cools from hot to brisk. Animals large and small come out of hiding. Instead of crunching leaves and dry moss under foot, my soft footfalls would be muffled by wet moss and wet ground. I could sneak up on a myriad of animals: squirrels, skunks, millipedes, deer, field mice, ground hogs. Because the rain washed my human scent from my clothes and boots, and my rain poncho changed my profile, I became just another creature in the woods.

SPRING

I loved early spring when the wild flowers started blooming. Of course, that also meant it was wildfire weather and there would be long hours of working and being on call 24-7. Fast, erratic winds, lots of dry leaves and dry grasses meant wildfire danger and fire control responsibility for the several weeks until the oak leaves were "the size of a squirrel's ear" signifying the end of fire season. Still it was beautiful to see the woods wake up from winter.

One day I walked up on a clutch of warm turkey eggs, so the hen must have been watching nearby. Another time I surprised a buck deer hiding behind a brush pile; I don't know who was more surprised. Another time I walked up on a squirrel sitting on top of a big mushroom eating an acorn. He must have been deaf, or hungry enough to not care.

The wildflowers of spring are so beautiful. Spring beauties and bloodroot would carpet the woodland hillsides. Brown trilliums would have their turn. In the valleys, Dutchman's britches with their funny white flowers and delicate foliage would joyfully greet me, along with clusters of bluebells, as I crossed creeks and valleys. Of course the varieties of flower species would change as I moved from north-facing slopes to south-facing slopes. Spring wildflowers had to grab the opportunity to reproduce before trees leafed out. Occasionally I saw Jack-in-the-pulpit or white trillium. Mayapples were common and sometimes harbored morel mushrooms. Soon the heavy timber on north slopes would leaf out stealing the sunlight, and it would be over for the year.

On south slopes, too much sunlight will heat things up. Delicate blossoms that missed their window of opportunity would get fried or die of thirst as refreshing early morning dews would evaporate. There are such a variety of wildflowers. Edgar Denison's book <u>Missouri Wildflowers</u> has been the pocket bible for many enthusiasts. For me Steyermark's <u>Flora of Missouri</u> is just too weighty.

Sassafras tree sprouts were easy to find to make that popular spring remedy: sassafras tea. Look on dry, rocky southwest slopes and find a sprout with dead sprouts attached, and you can usually pull up a thick sassafras root to make lots of tea.

SUMMER

I remember when I was caught in a summer storm near Meramec State Park on a wooded ridge. The timber was not extraordinarily large though as a precaution because of lightning I dropped my metal keys and belt buckle near a tree and moved off to watch the lightning show, resigned to getting sopping wet. The lightning flashed and the thunder rolled. The rain came down hard, restricting my vision. The storm raged on. If I had been a sponge I would have exploded. As quickly as it came the storm passed so I retrieved my keys and belt buckle and moved on. The sun came out and I saw wisps of vapor rising from the forest floor as the late afternoon sun warmed the ground evaporating the rain water. I caught the fresh scent of a fox. By the time I finished cruising the timber my clothes were dried out, and so were my field notes.

One of my favorite experiences happened in Gasconade County. I was checking timber in a light drizzle. Trees were pretty thin on a dry rocky ridgetop. Wearing a long poncho to cover my cruising notes must have made me look like some weird shrub, because a spotted deer fawn bounced up so close I could have touched it. Totally oblivious of my presence it lifted its back leg to scratch its ear; I could see gnats flying around its ears. Then it bounced over in front of me, shook its head, stood for a few moments, and then bounced off. I stood there and watched it go. It was just another beautiful day.

Though hot as blazes, hiking through the woods could be made more comfortable by standing in a creek. The cold water would soak through the heavy leather and thick socks. Wearing high boots was necessary for me hiking through brushy woods and uneven, obstacle-filled terrain. Poisonous snakes could strike at exposed ankles. Support helps prevent ankle sprains. The wet leather sure kept my feet cool for some time. I'm blessed my feet were tough and didn't develop blisters.

Once I walked up on a water moccasin sunning itself in an opening in the woods. It was obviously unruffled by my presence, so I decided to back away quietly. Seeing snakes was not particularly common for me. They were certainly there, but I didn't go looking for trouble and they had plenty warning. I was usually pretty noisy so I rarely saw snakes, or deer or turkey.

Considering the intense heat and high humidity of Missouri summers, the gnats buzzing around my ears, and ticks and mosquitoes with their threatening diseases, summer was certainly not my favorite time of year. But it is my favorite time for free food. Coral mushrooms are everywhere on ridges and slopes, and in my frying pan. Bramble fruits are available, like blackberries, raspberries, and dewberries. And they were mighty tasty on a hot day. Blackberries I have found in the open and abundant, but their thorny branches often draw blood and won't let go of my pants. Raspberries were uncommon, but very, very sweet.

Though blooming in spring, the fruits of the abundant may apples [not an apple] become edible in early summer, as they turn from green to yellow. They can be tasty on a hot, dry day. Another flower I enjoyed was wild ginger growing on rich, low northeast slopes. The flower, is dark brown and forms in spring at ground level to attract crawling pollinators. But the clusters of heart-shaped, dark green leaves are attractive in summer. Gooseberry shrubs were common in overgrazed, acidic woodlands. And I mostly found blueberries on south and west slopes where fewer trees opened space for the short shrubs. To reduce thirst, I would break off twigs of sassafras and chew on them for awhile.

Low-growing dewberries were sometimes available, but I got in very big trouble with one once. Earlier, I saw what I believed to be the death cap mushroom which is a member of the *Amanita* genus. Stupidly I touched it. I knew better than to touch a strange mushroom, but I did. It was awhile later while inspecting timber for a land owner, I spotted a dewberry and popped it in my mouth, continuing on my way. Suddenly my head felt like it was going to explode. I dropped to my knees and just held on to my head. The internet said some people use these as hallucinogens, but I had no spinning or wild pictures or "cozy little trip". It was purely intense pain. I was just crouched over hoping my head would not explode. Thank God after awhile my head stopped throbbing and I could stand up and hike to the car, smarter for the experience, and that was plenty enough.

Actually the *Amanita* is good for trees; it is a mycorrhizal fungus. Mycorrhizae form a symbiotic relationship with the tree's roots. The fungus grows in or on roots of plants. It sends out extensive slender, root-like structures which absorb water and nutrients from the soil and trade these for food in the form of carbon. In soils that are too alkaline or acidic for the plant it can alter the chemistry of the nutrient to make it more palatable for the trees and other plants. Growing in or around roots, it can protect trees from invading harmful bacteria, other fungi, or other organisms. The mushroom is the fruiting body of the fungus. It comes to the surface to spread its spores around to reproduce itself.

AUTUMN

Autumn meant a changing of the rhythm of the forest. Hormonal changes cause leaves to lose food-making chlorophyll. The green pigments that cover the reds and golds are lost, freeing an explosion of color. Awe-inspiring panoramas are all over Missouri, for weeks. The internet suggests some attractive drives. Although if you get a county road map and look for curvy roads south and west of St. Louis, you will be rewarded.

But probably the most exquisite details are in the designs on individual leaves. Often the veins stand out with a strong color separate from the interior of the leaf. Or the leaf may be marbled, like the colors in a fireworks display. Intensity and degree of reds, purples, and pinks depend on warm days and cold nights. Tree species and varieties are factors, but soil has control. Dry, rocky south and west slopes can be wildly colorful. The individual leaves deserve to be framed. Yellows are typical of hickories, ginkos, and many maples, but the intensity of the tree color can be breathtaking. The leaves themselves tend to be a solid color, but they seem to glow.

Though heavy rains sometimes hurry things along, usually leaves linger for a colorful sequence of changes led by poison ivy vines and finished by Missouri oaks. Abscisic acid hormones cause the leaves to cleanly break away from the tree as they gracefully drift to the ground, providing nutrients and cover for the next generation of trees. Dry leaves fuel fall fire season in Missouri. Though less dramatic than spring fire season, the smoke of fires fills the air. Often people are burning leaves on their property and the fires escape into the woods.

Trees again reveal their naked limbs in all their beauty as they turn chemicals in the tissues under their bark into their own form of anti-freeze to prepare for winter.

Fall also meant my favorite fruits might be available, if I could beat the animals to the pawpaw... questionable at best. Serviceberry trees (*Amelanchier arborea)* were everywhere in the woods, but as a forester I never could find a fruit until I retired and volunteered at the Missouri Botanical Garden where I found them. No wonder the animals didn't share. In Franklin County, I walked into a large patch of goldenseal. I probably wouldn't have noticed it, but the abundant seeds were striking. If the medicinal herb hunters knew about it that patch of goldenseal would disappear, but I certainly didn't breathe a word.

WINTER

Winter is special too. It makes measuring and evaluating trees much easier. Winter is easier to deal with than summer humidity and bugs.

I do remember a particularly cold time, well below freezing. I was checking timber in a valley with good views of some large white oaks. The sun was warming the tree trunks. Suddenly I heard a very loud bang. But where did it come from? Then I heard another, and another. I finally realized what was happening. Frost cracks were popping open on the trees. I have seen frost cracks on trees and probably heard them pop before, but this was dramatic. It made me think of Tchaikovsky's 1812 Overture. Frost cracks usually don't become infected, probably because it is winter and the cracks seal up again with the natural expansion of cell tissues in warmer weather. But it was loud! And my feet were certainly cold. But the experience was worth it.

Recognizing trees in winter is so much easier than in summer. The twigs at the end of branches have buds, leaf scars, bud scale scars, breathing holes called lenticels, maybe thorns or thorn-like projections, hairs, and color. The buds usually have scales, though each tree species is different. Buds may be sharp pointed like [hard] sugar maple and the red oak group, or rounded like the white oak group, or frayed like [soft] silver maple and box elder, which is also a maple. Box elder also has very, very bright green twigs. Like other maples, buds are on opposite sides of the branch, unlike oaks which are alternating.

Black oak buds are so fuzzy they look white. Of course, red and black oaks and others in that group are so closely related that they inter-breed with each other—hybridize. That makes their progeny difficult to identify. Sometimes hair may, instead of being soft like on persimmon buds, be short and stiff like on ash. Cottonwood buds may be sort of sticky–resinous. Most trees have a bud at the end of the branch, but on some the bud comes out at an angle, giving a zigzag appearance to the branch, like honeylocust, redbud, and sycamore (plane tree). This is called a pseudo-terminal bud.

To confuse things, some buds have only 2 scales like basswood (lindens), some only 1 like sycamore, some have none visible like honeylocust. Ash buds have no visible scales, but the tissues are covered by rusty brown short stubbly hairs. Bitternut hickory buds are also naked (no scale) but covered by soft sulfur yellow hairs. This is vastly different from the other hickories which are definitely scaled and often quite large. Pawpaw buds have soft dark brown hairs and poison ivy has soft ivory colored hairs...trust me. Black walnut's bud is also naked and protected by soft creamy hairs, and they may have a mustache under the buds. The leaf scars form a happy face by its shape and location of the bundle scars. And the pith on the stem is chambered and chocolate brown. If you scrape the outer bark on a large walnut, it is a soft chocolate brown. The ash's inner bark is a soft cream color. That's a great way to recognize them in winter if you can't see the twigs, because they both have diamond-patterns in the bark. Of course so does bitternut hickory, but its inner bark is hard as stone.

I could go on and on. Can you see why I love naked trees. The trees tell the story of their past life, of competition for sunlight, written in their limbs and branches. The healthy tree overproduces, providing pollen for bees which assures the tree's reproduction, fruit for squirrels and birds and people, leaves for insects and deer, carbon when discarded parts are decomposed by soil organisms such as worms, protozoa, and soil bacteria (good stuff), as well as carbon through its roots. We don't really understand how the forest community works together, but it is profound. Nectar-producing flowers that grow on forest soils attract predatory insects that eat the insects that eat the trees. Wow!

Of course flowering trees like dogwoods and pawpaws provide nectar for butterflies, bees and flies. Large trees provide homes and protection for raccoons and owls. Pawpaw is linked to the attractive zebra swallowtail. The parts of the forest—the north slope, south slope, ridgetop, ravine, bottomland—work together to form a cohesive unit in the forest. Different micro-environments support a host of different species of animals and insects. Each is home to hoards of different insects which are food for different animals, which are food for different animals. Helping land owners to recognize these different environments and then to adjust their management to protect their forest, and improve their forest, was very rewarding, and very challenging.

"…The woods are lovely, dark and deep,
But I have promises to keep,
And miles to go before I sleep,
And miles to go before I sleep."
ROBERT FROST "Stopping by Woods on a Snowy Evening"

"When I pass to my reward
Whatever that may be,
I'd like my friends to think of me
As one who loved a tree...."
SAMUEL N. BAXTER "I LOVE A TREE"

CHAPTER 4

The Magnificent Tree

THE TREE IS AN AMAZING organism. It is no wonder its symbolic shape is represented in so many facets of our lives. A mechanical wonder, it can extract water and nutrients from the ground horizontally, 2½ times the tree's vertical height. Assuming mycorrhizae have attached themselves to the roots, an additional 30' are possible. [Information and images can be found on the web.] The tree transports water against gravity up to leaves on the tip of the tree driven by simple evapo-transpiration, because sunlight and dry winds evaporate water from the leaf surfaces.

Leaf water is drawn through leaf petioles from twigs which draw water from branches which draw water from the trunk which draws water through the flare from the roots. Trees such as yellow-poplar, in the original natural Missouri forest, could grow 100 feet tall, but historically have been known to grow 200 feet. That's a lot of gravitational pull! When things get really hot this system all but shuts down because the little "mouths" on the backs (undersides) of leaves called stomates close in response to hot, dry weather and hormonal activity in the leaves.

Leaf water and atmospheric carbon dioxide are combined with the energy from sunlight in the cell's chloroplast. The chlorophyll factory turns these ingredients into starch, a fuel that energizes the system. Some of the starch is used to defend the tree, some to repair damage, some to grow, and some to transport materials to provide for the tree's insatiable need for water and nutrients. Starch is stored behind the buds for next spring's leaf expansion, and in roots for root expansion, and twigs, and wherever. Loss of any of these body parts is tragic. When trees must use stored food for extended periods of time due to weather or defense or competition etc., the tree gets stressed.

Insects are constantly looking for weakened individuals. When an insect tries to invade a healthy tree it will be blocked by defense chemicals. If the tree is weak, the insect attacks will likely be successful. Fast-growing trees can be particularly vulnerable because they are too busy growing to defend themselves. How much damage is done depends on the insect, and on the disease pathogens that invade the open wound. Some invading diseases do initial attack, and others invade weakened tissues and further the decay process.

Each tree species has evolved different techniques for providing for its health and nutrition and for defending itself against insects, diseases, mammals, and lawnmowers. Chemicals in the leaf such as phenols are a typical example. Even thorny, modified branches along the trunks of honeylocust are a protective adaptation. Based on its vigor (genetics) and vitality (environment-based) the individual tree is able to make new adaptations for survival that may be passed on improving species survival. Research has discovered that trees communicate. For example, when trees are attacked, surrounding trees respond by producing leaves that are tougher with a lower nutritional content.

Considerable research on soils and nutrition has opened our minds to multiple ways trees have of defending themselves, such as producing alcohols and ethanols and other chemicals poisonous to insects trying to feed on them. Compartmentalizing damage and the fungi and bacterias invading wound sites with chemical barriers was explained by Dr. Alex Shigo and referred to as CODIT (Compartmentalization of Decay In Trees). Dr. Shigo is particularly known for his pictures and diagrams of the internal tissues of branch collars and wound responses related to the atrocious practices of "flush-cut pruning" and "topping". Though he died October 2006, his legacy will live on forever in his books, articles and photos.

Dr. Kim Coder is another who has produced much information on nitrogen movement in soil and in plants as well as related research on tree survival in urban environments. Governments, universities, and private industry, such as Dr. John Ball, Ms. Nelda Matheny, Dr. Bruce Fraedrich, Kent State and other university research, The Davey Tree Expert and Asplundh Tree Expert companies, Minnesota's Dept.

of Natural Resources and others have provided studies on construction damage, hazard trees, planting, etc. And this is only the beginning.

The tree lives in a community of flowers, grasses, mushrooms, shrubs, other trees, insects, lizards & amphibians, mammals, and people. The tree itself is a community of lichens, funguses, insects, owls, squirrels, birds, and many other organisms that depend on the tree for food and shelter. All the parts cooperate to aid in survival. The tree's roots absorb oxygen and give off carbon dioxide into the soil in their process of respiration. But the tree's leaves absorb carbon dioxide (and other pollutants) from the air and give off oxygen which we use. All this work takes energy. Energy is necessary to lift water to the leaves and move the food leaves produce to all the other parts.

Many "beneficials" exist in the environment. Most obvious are predatory insects, such as the delicate appearing lacewings and the colorful ladybugs and their hungry larvae which eat the insects that eat plant leaves. But many others exist such as beneficial funguses and soil bacterias.

Strength counts, but endurance prevails. Strength is measured by the ability to survive regardless of the challenges. But species survival depends on reproduction. It is recognized that trees that are stressed put extra energy into reproduction...a lot! Think about that before you consider topping your sweetgum. It's better to fertilize, mulch, aerate and do other cultural things to help your tree. Research has shown that trees touching each other are healthier.

I admire the trees' power and strength, their endurance, their tenacity, and their individuality. I feel at peace when among trees. I know most of the local tree species by name and consider them friends and teachers. In the evolution of things, trees and plants might outlive people, though we have made worldwide considerable changes in the environment. People have in our short time on the earth, destroyed plant communities that have evolved for millions of years. When we are gone, or hopefully evolved into something less destructive, the forest will do what it seems to do best: Adapt.

Many times I lay down beneath a tree and looked up to admire what I could only interpret as strength, tenacity, and a will to live that goes beyond understanding. I admit I would first check for soundness of the trunk and absence of dead or structurally unsound branches above me. This tree is a black gum on a north slope overlooking the Meramec River. I also remember the bend in the river and the gravel bar below this tree. For black gum being sound is notable, since most black gums I have seen in the forest were in woodlands burned by old forest fires. Being a fast-growing tree they may look big healthy, but often they would have hollow hearts. Black gums are also beautiful in autumn with their rich red leaves. But keep the lawn mowers away from them.

Life Principles I Have Learned From Trees:

Hold your ground against the flood of stressors that come against you.

Where there is one leader, it can grow straight and strong. When there are multiple leaders, they struggle against each other, forcing all to grow apart from each other.

What works in one location, may weaken in another. Change and adapt.

If your root foundation is strong, you will rise again.

To grow, you must produce, reach out, and expand into new territory.

To weather hard times, you must sacrifice.

To be strong and hold against the winds of change, you must stay active and develop muscle.

Patience...it takes time to grow.

Don't complain about your neighbors...just aim higher. Often they bring out the best in you.

When you are blocked, break the obstruction, grow over it, or grow in another direction.

When bad things happen, make changes

Reach out in all directions to stabilize yourself and absorb the water, oxygen, and nutrients you need to be strong.

To be healthy, you must be aware of all your body's needs and provide appropriately.

When things get hot...keep your mouth shut. (Stomates, which resemble lips, control evaporation of moisture from plants.)

You depend on the community for health and support. If you overproduce and help the community, the community can better provide for your needs.

If you injure yourself, infection can follow. Decay may grow in your heart. Health will decline and parts may drop off.

Fast growers do not take time and energy to build defenses. Slow growers tend to live longer, healthier lives because of it.

Some environments are beneficial; and some are not.

Know your resources. When under attack, you will need to defend yourself.

When you lose one of your parts, the other parts must compensate.

When you are badly broken, reinvest. The results may be surprising.

To be healthy, you must get all the essential elements in proper amounts.

When you have a hollow heart you are structurally weak.

You can live for decades with a disease eating away at your heart, but it can destroy your body.

Survival of the species rules.

The greatest hazard in life is to risk nothing. Those who avoid risk may avoid suffering and sorrow, but they cannot learn, feel, change, grow, love and live.
AUTHOR UNKNOWN

CHAPTER 5

The Novice Forester

A S A STATE FORESTER AVAILABLE to serve the public, landowners would call and make an appointment with me. We would meet on the land and walk the land observing trees and the plant community. This time would also give me the opportunity to understand the landowners' needs and desires.

To be an effective forester I believed I had to change how I presented myself to landowners, such as speaking with a deeper voice and using body language and gestures that were a bit more masculine. When working with land owners I would occasionally have to take long strides, and a few land owners have tried to out-walk me in the woods. Of course, I was in great shape working in the woods every day and knew how to comfortably cover ground in the woods. After the land owner tired, we could begin to discuss their forest resource. Then we could work on recognizing their assets and plan the work ahead to improve their resources.

Being available to help people recognize the value and potential of their forest was rewarding. I always enjoyed finding work for land owners. And there was always much work to do to repair their woodlands from the scars of past management practices. It may take decades, even generations, to bring a forest back to health. It is good to know people heard and responded by making an effort to improve the health of their forest.

Land owners all treated me with respect. Many had a set purpose such as to sell timber, but most just wanted to understand their forest better. Some were local farmers and land owners, but the majority were absentee land owners from St. Louis (people who owned but did not live on their land). Generally, land was owned by a man and wife team. Perhaps because I was a woman the wife came also. I like to think I have inspired the wives to feel more comfortable in the woods, perhaps less challenged and more understanding of the role trees play in our lives. A few even embraced the National Tree Farm System.

Having them both there allowed a more complete understanding of their forest resource. Men and women seem to have different perspectives, and different goals. Many men and women were hunters and wanted to manage for deer and turkey. But even with dedicated hunters, suggesting plants for butterflies and other wildlife appealed to them. Helping them to recognize the majesty of the trees as they adapt to, and change their environment was very rewarding. Growing up in St. Louis perhaps made my relating to absentee land owners easier. But my love for the land also made it easier for me to work with people who lived on the land.

If I was marking their timber in preparation for a sale, I generally insisted the landowner be with me. This not only protected me from inadvertently crossing unmarked boundary lines, but it gave me more time to spend with the land owner, demonstrating how to achieve our goals, discussing sale topics such as suggesting designated routes for log skidders, loading areas for logging trucks, and communicating with loggers. Besides, it helped to have someone tally (record numbers) while I measured and sprayed paint on trees to mark them. And it made judging my location while marking timber easier in areas without strong landmarks.

When marking timber I carried a variety of tools including a hatchet with a wooden handle and flat side for thumping on trees to check trees for soundness (similar to sounding a wall for studs). The sounds define whether a tree was solid or hollow, or both, but much more. Sound can locate pockets of decay in otherwise solid trunks. You can follow seams of weakness coming from the roots or from a wound. You can note changes in density related to growing conditions. Environment, species, bark thicknesses, slope location, rain-saturated bark etc. alter the sound. It works in the city also, but echoes off houses, buildings or walls complicate the sound.

Other tools were the historical Biltmore Stick (images available on the web), for measuring diameter and estimating height. Veneer tree measurements require more sophisticated equipment such as diameter tapes. Height would be estimated closer because the butt log, the bottom log, may be all that would qualify for high-grade veneer, depending on growing conditions. Veneer was most often white oak. At the mill, veneer logs may be sliced, or rolled, to remove thin sheets of wood tissue. These sheets can be found on high quality furniture or plywood. In Missouri, individual white oak trees could sell for several hundred dollars. Red oaks could also be high quality and may be used for flooring or furniture.

And then there is black walnut. Historically, most walnut was removed for gun stocks during the Civil War, but walnut is growing back. Veneer for furniture, and gunstocks, commands some respectable prices. Probably the highest prices I cooperated on were on logs being removed illegally from some rich Missouri River bottomland. The would-be thieves got their log skidder stuck in the mud trying to get the logs out and were caught by a neighboring land owner. I believe each tree commanded over a thousand dollars, though they might have received much more with a proper sale.

Sawtimber was estimated in 16 foot (log) increments. Prices were not terribly high and needed large numbers of trees to justify a sale. Cost of moving equipment for logging is a major expense. But if marked judiciously, and logged carefully, a sale should be good for the land owner, the forest resource and the logger.

When working alone, measuring distance for cruising timber (judging tree quality and quantity based on a calculated number of sample plots), my pace measured at about five feet. In order to locate sample plots to be made in the woods at locations laid out on a flat topographic map, measuring distances in the woods was somewhat complicated by steep and changing slopes, obstructions like down trees, and impassable areas. The topographic map would allow for adjustments.

I cannot leave forestry without expressing my respect for loggers. I had not met a logger who, with life and limb, I would not trust in the woods. And I have spent time with them before and during sales. Cutting timber is a most dangerous profession. I would suggest caution when finalizing sale management and finances. They have expensive equipment and employees and families to care for.

Logging is very, very dangerous. "Hung trees" are challenging and dangerous. "Barber chairs", also called "tombstones", are less frequent but very unpredictable as the falling tree splits and spins out of control. And of course there are unsound trees and "widow makers". You can find these terms and pictures on the web. Lumber prices can change somewhat unpredictably affecting income when a truckload of logs is delivered to the mill. In the crush of time, somehow a tree, or even a truckload, may not be accounted for.

If you are a landowner selling timber, do your research. Know your logger, and the sawmills. "Extreme Logger" viewed on Discovery channel may help you relate to the business of logging. I particularly recommend viewing on the Discovery channel the veneer buyer logging with mules pulling the cut trees to the truck for loading. In Missouri, we still have a few skilled mule loggers, and they typically are less damaging to residual timber where selective logging is the goal (selecting individual trees for removal and leaving the residual trees for years later).

I remember when I first started work as a forester I was told I would need to spend probably three or four days a week in the woods. Somewhat intimidating at first, I quickly found myself in the woods every day. I even did my paperwork in the woods, or in the car looking at the woods. After a few years, the District Forester, Mr. Woodland, prevailed on me to work in the office one day per week. But any excuse to get out of the office was great.

I miss the work. If I could, I would go back in a heartbeat. You could see God's work in the trees with their flowing branches reaching for the sun. You could see His work in every leaf which supports the forest community. I really felt a part of the forest though I was only a visitor.

*What lies behind us and what lies before us are tiny
matters compared to what lies within us.*
OLIVER WENDEL HOLMES

CHAPTER 6

Wild Fire Fighting

THE ADRENALIN RUSH IS UNDENIABLE. The heat of the fire causes whirls of fire that dance across hard fought fire lines on a whim of the wind. The closure when the fire is finally contained is great, but it could rekindle and cross the line that night, or even days later. I also had the exciting opportunity to fight fires in California, Montana, and New Mexico. It is all hot, dirty, dangerous, exciting work.

One summer of college, May to August 1977, I applied and was accepted by the U.S. Department of Agriculture, Forest Service, as a forestry aide. I was sent to the Angeles National Forest in Southern California to work with a fire crew on a 4-wheel drive fire truck. The forestry class I had on fire weather perhaps helped qualify me for the position. Where Missouri's fire seasons are spring and fall, California's is summer.

It was interesting to note the similarities in forestry. For example, a northeast slope will have thicker and taller timber; a southwest slope, being hotter and dryer, is typically more sparsely timbered. Part time, I cruised some plantations for seedling survival. When planting seedlings, the attention to planting techniques affects survival regardless of location. I also noted that California's rattlesnakes are considerably larger than Missouri's.

Working there with a crew on a 4-wheel drive fire truck, I saw back country and mountains of remarkable beauty. I also saw charred north slopes where tall, broad pines had been reduced to blackened toothpicks, and where the ash underfoot was a foot thick and billowed up as I walked, burying my boots. Nothing would hold the soil turned to ash when rains would inevitably come.

We drove out of state east across the desert to New Mexico in our very hot fire truck to work on the Radio fire (large fires were given names). Our crew had laid hoses reaching a mile from the fire truck. We had dug and scraped a clear line along this length and had put in laterals to wait on the hillside for the fire to back down to us. In this location it worked well, but it got scary when a fire fighting plane dropped a load of fire retardant on our fire truck. Being perhaps a mile away and guarding the line, we saw the plane drop the retardant and then our hose went dead, suddenly losing water. Retardant is hard on trucks, so we were without water for awhile as the truck got a bath. I've also eaten more military rations than I had wished, but never complained...much.

I spent many hours sharpening our Mattox pick-axes: good axes with a grub hoe on the back side of the axe (see it on the web). Weight and balance were good for swinging, but I certainly used the hoe more than the axe. And after every fire you gathered your equipment before it had a chance to disappear.

Years later as a forester, about 1982, I went with our fire crews from Missouri, to assist with a fire in Montana. I saw claw marks high on a tree trunk that caused me chills. I jumped out of a helicopter onto a razorback ridge so narrow the helicopter could not land, the ridge was narrower than the copter's skids. And it was all downhill from there, literally. The country was wild and beautiful with lots of trees and very few roads.

FIRE FIGHTING MISSOURI STYLE

Forest fire fighting in the 21st century is certainly considerably different than in the early 1980s when I became intimately familiar with the techniques. Urban homeowners moving to the country are building bigger and more expensive homes. Getting homeowner's insurance without a fire department is difficult. This alone has forced changes. Volunteer fire departments have become more sophisticated and better equipped with some paid staff.

In the deep woods, where roads or even rough woods trails didn't exist, we were it. You can put out a lot of fire with a good broom rake with a tough hickory handle. With a good swing of the rake [power-raking] and a 3-person crew you can clear a good line ahead of a fire. You had to leave enough room between the control line and the fire in order to put in a backfire. That would depend on slope direction and steepness of the terrain, wind direction and speed, humidity, fuels (dead leaves, dead grasses, other plant growth, etc.), and how many hours of raking you had already put in that day, and just how fast that fire head was traveling.

Lighting a backfire is the technique of fighting fire with fire. You clear part of a line ahead of the advancing wild fire. Then as part of the crew continues building clear line, the last member of the crew lights the backfire. The backfire will hopefully move in quick enough to meet the advancing wild fire. Though somewhat primitive, the broom rake is also effective for spreading the backfire. You don't want to light more backfire than you can protect. The wind can jump backwards, crossing your control line. I've seen whirls of fire cross over the line. A fire whirl is like a miniature tornado made of fire and flaming debris forming from the ground up.

The backfire burns to the oncoming fire, thus the fire goes out because it runs out of fuel. Of course a wind can get sneaky and blow a spark to the next ridge ahead of the fire, which means you lose your battle line. After scouting the new burn area, you go back to where the line held and begin again...and again and again. Then, of course, someone has to go back to check that a tree has not fallen over the line or scout for problem trees.

Missouri counties have been frequently burned over the past decades, when open range was legal in Missouri. Landowners bought animals based on what they could afford to buy rather than how much land they had to feed them. They let their animals roam at will on public and private lands. To ensure grass to eat, they would burn the woods, stringing fires in various ways.

Trees that are burned by fires often become hollow with open catfaces--archways into the tree's damaged interior. [If you put the words 'fire', 'tree', 'catface' into the internet you can get some pretty impressive images.] These trees can burn from the inside out, throwing sparks out of holes in high branches.

There is a real sense of accomplishment putting fires out. Some days, and nights, are high hazard. When humidity is low and winds high, cigarettes, escaped trash fires, firebugs (incendiary), can easily start a fire. We might go to 4 or 5 on a bad day, maybe even an all-nighter. I have been on several. I was just a small part of a system begun years ago when the department was formed. Fire fighters are dedicated and work many hard hours.

Whenever the weather was seriously threatening–dry and windy in spring and fall–we worked or were on call 24-7 waiting for the inevitable. One spring we went six weeks without a day off...finally it rained! One year spring fire season went well into summer; the humidity created by evaporating moisture from leaf surfaces was not enough. As a result of the drought, the following spring forest trees showed serious "staghorning" where the tops of trees never leafed out.

Control of wildfires in Missouri dates back to1938. Meramec Forest District was one of the first four fire districts formed years ago in Missouri. As a forester we fought fires with the fire crews. Fighting fires was hot work demanding much time and energy. It was hard work, the smoke chocked your breathing, steam fogged your goggles, your muscles were numb, and then you went on for just a few hours more. If you are curious, you might check Missouri Department of Conservation history on the web.

Serving landowners and fighting fires often came into competition for time and energy. But as a forester you recognize the damage resulting from fires years/decades after the fire(s) and the need to stop this damage to trees. When the fire is out, it's out...maybe.

You knew those trees outside the burned area were safe, at least until the next fire. We had a firebug operating in a remote area on the district, so all-night fires were not unique. There is something interesting about seeing the sun come up on your way home from a fire. There is something also beautiful, though somewhat eerie, about driving to a fire in the dark of night. The "V"-shaped wedges of fire that creep down hillsides, the sparks flying from a hollow tree burning like a chimney, the tornado-like fire whirls, all are beautiful in their way.

The employees who fight the fires for days, and nights, during fire seasons, are admirable. Their dedication, their professionalism, their unselfishness are virtues beyond compare. There is a book in every one of these individuals who dedicate their lives to benefit our forests.

Going out to meet a land owner the next morning after an all-night fire was tough. You just shower, change clothes and keep moving. I admit I did enjoy firefighting some, and I was in really, really great shape those days despite the m.s. When I wasn't working I was riding my horse before or after work or cutting firewood. By the late '80s the m.s. was affecting my stamina, and it was time for a change. Firefighting needs people at their peak, and I was over that.

WIDOW MAKERS

The term probably comes from loggers who worked felling timber when a branch would suddenly break off, fall, and kill someone. If an area is frequently burned, say every 10 years or so or more frequently, the battle scars are obvious on the trees. Wounds at the base particularly on the high side of trees on hillsides show arches of wound tissue starting at ground level where the tree tried to grow around a wound. The wound happens when a fire is moving up a hill. It gets to a tree and wraps around a tree on both sides, meeting on the high side, there fire meets fire.

And, of course, the wounded interior wood decays. A progression of diseases spread up the interior of the tree's trunk and out the branches. Hollow trees with hollow branches don't sell well, so they try to cut them before the tree hollows out. Most loggers are smart enough to not stand under these trees, a big branch with a hollow core can break and fall. But it can be hard to see, especially with a full crown of leaves.

However, maybe the fires were not so frequent, but became hot enough to seriously wound some trees. Time passes. In 20 years the wound tissue trying to cover the wound may come together. A vigorous growing tree can hide the wound to even experienced loggers, and foresters. That is why we foresters carried hatchets with a flat side. By thumping on the tree you can discover hidden defects. The fun part was finding a really big tree in a crowd of young trees. You hit it hard with the hatchet's flat side and the 'bonggggg' can echo in the hills. But don't hang around too long.

I have seen stumps after a sale where the tree was open and hollow at the base, but up at 4 feet above the ground the tree was solid and marketable timber, especially white oaks. Or maybe a tree is solid, but disease got in at a high hole where a flying ember got caught between branches. Widow makers come in many sizes.

Here I should add that other things can damage the base, opening a tree to decay...like lawnmowers and string trimmers! Widow makers can fall in city parks, and campgrounds, and parking lots....

I heard this on a Christian music recording: "Satan is a liar, and he can start a fire."

I would rather be exposed to the inconveniences attending too much liberty than those attending too small a degree of it.
THOMAS JEFFERSON

CHAPTER 7

Surprise: Multiple Sclerosis

BUT THERE IS YET A demon, the multiple sclerosis. What will it
bring tomorrow?

So what is courage? I find it takes courage to get up in the
morning. My legs won't work. It takes courage to go to bed at night,
not knowing whether the strange nauseating vibrations or muscle
spasms would wake me up again; knowing that my pads and towels
will get soaked with urine and that would wake me. No doubt that my
living water will flow, and flow, and flow. Will I have the strength to
face another day's crises. It doesn't really matter whether a person has
courage or not. The next day is going to come anyway. Put heart and
soul into each day. Do for others, but take care of yourself. God did
not create selfish, egotistical wimps. We are to do the best we can to do
the best we can. We are to love others as God loves them. And we are
to love ourselves as God loves us.

The quote "That which does not kill you makes you stronger." by
Friedrich Nietzsche, "Twilight of the Idols", was posted on the wall at
the gym at Meramec Community College where I took karate. I also
found it in a *Time* magazine article about Nelson Mandela. Twenty
seven years in prison enduring the most awesome deprivations only
made him stronger. According to the article, Mr. Mandela saw himself
not as a savior but as an ordinary man confronting extraordinary
circumstances.

In 1983, I was diagnosed with multiple sclerosis. Not only was I a "female" forester, but I was a female forester with M.S. To be put on probation 6 years later at the age of 42 was traumatic. To leave the woods for a sedentary life, was shocking, scary, and very threatening. Emotionally I fell apart.

I survived rejection, low self esteem and guilt for having M.S. I learned too late, when a supervisor tries to get rid of you, don't take it personally and get a good attorney. Why does it take a traumatic event to wake up? I didn't heal, and probably never will, but like trees, I sealed. I compartmentalized the wound. Life goes on.

I hope this book will help others avoid my mistakes. Life is a journey; growth is often painful. However, if you have m.s. please read on with an open mind and positive attitude. Everyone's m.s. is different. You probably will not suffer to the extreme I am. New medicines can help in the early stages. I pray you will be strong against this disease.

I don't know how much more fun I can stand. The m.s. impacts everything I try to do. The bladder is totally unpredictable! The progression from unpredictable, through bowel and bladder dysfunction, to current vulnerability and two loads of laundry a day for pads and towels is dreadful. What will tomorrow bring. It is only a question of when. When will I need full time nursing care and a catheter. When will I be forced into a nursing home? I'm told I should have care 24-7, but so far I have avoided it.

Covering the scooter seat with plastic packaging tape waterproofed it and prevented leaks through the scooter seat to the carpet, for awhile. I have lots of towels. And I am always grateful when the rug cleaners come. But I found a new trick. A bottle of anti-bacterial dish soap and water, poured on the rug and covered with a pad overnight does a remarkable job of cleaning.

I've gone from walking with a cane, to a walker, to a scooter, and a van with a lift to a conversion van in just the last few years, and it keeps getting worse. It is scary. I miss so much but I have given up grieving, and driving. It's just another day. I've had this since at least 1983, but since I returned to the city and don't get the exercise, it has moved faster. Lack of exercise like walking up and down hills is a factor, but age probably is also. I'm over 60 now. But it isn't much compared to my mother who died at 98. Pop died prematurely at 92. Longevity with this disease is really scary.

I tell you these things not because I want your pity. There doesn't seem to be anything here on earth that can stop this continual challenge of dealing with this disease, progressive multiple sclerosis, 24 hours a day. I guess I've tried most everything except bee stings, which are not safe to use alone.

There is the nutritional product, Reliv, that I started with in 2006. For many who started with this early, the m.s. has gone into remission. It has helped me with the bladder and bowel problems, Thank God. I use this exclusively for food. In fact I don't need to cook, and I shop mostly for fruit and dark chocolate, mmm. My recent blood test brought glowing praise from my doctor who I continue to surprise with perfect blood pressure and good health except for stress and m.s. And that's enough.

Have I ever considered suicide? at least once a day. I probably would, but I believe in a merciful God. I believe He has paradise waiting for me. He created life, and would not appreciate my treating it so lightly. God has given me much joy and peace in the midst of this diabolical disease. However, fear of the Lord is for real. Hell is for real. He suffered and died for me that I might have life. Offering up my suffering for souls who don't know Him as I have come to know Him, is the least I can do.

All right, it isn't all bad. It forced me to find something more important in life than running around in the woods. A friend dragged me, a fallen-away Catholic, to a Catholic Charismatic Mass. I had been away for decades. A month later I went back. The peace and joy I felt there was beyond belief or understanding. And the tears I shed would have filled the Great Salt Lake. They were healing tears. Can you relate?

Perhaps because of the struggles and pain with the loss of forestry, and with the m.s., God has been merciful enough to grant me many gifts. Knowledge and understanding have helped me come running back to God and has restored my childhood trust in Him. The multiple sclerosis is a horrendous burden. Yet I can sometimes find peace. I can go to the Charismatic Mass and find joy and peace and even laughter. In prayer I find joy.

That doesn't make the bad times easier. And the bad times can happen multiple times a day/night. I do get very frustrated and angry. And I don't mince words when letting God know exactly what I think of this disease. There is no doubt in my mind that Satan uses m.s. to come against and break me down, perhaps in ways saints of old were tortured. But I am no saint.

I can't make it alone. Things go wrong: the ramp, the van, the scooter, the toilet, the hospital bed, transferring to/from anything. Anything can happen at any time. I have called 911 numerous times and they have kindly and patiently extricated me from many situations. Thank God for 911. Friends have rescued me from many situations also, and helped me in so many ways. Friends sometimes take me to places I cannot go, and I am so grateful, for there is so much I miss.

All this boils down to one major realization: I cannot make it without His angels. And they come in many forms. Every day is a miracle. Oh, a big one would be great, but all the little miracles that happen each day are the reason I am here. The difference between me and normal people is I am forced to notice the miracles, but miracles are happening for you also. Every time you get in the car and make it to your destination safely, know that someone is looking out for you, someone is praying for you.

If you doubt miracles, study a tree, or as Professor Al Shigo would suggest "touch a tree". I don't suggest hugging a tree; all kinds of insects call trees home, and some bite.

The Wright Brothers flew right through the smoke screen of impossibility
CHARLES F. KETTERING

CHAPTER 8

Happy, Out On the Farm

IN 1983 I WAS DIAGNOSED with multiple sclerosis. I knew if I did not act immediately I would never accomplish my dream of living in the country with a horse. That year I rented a property north of Sullivan and bought a 2-year old untrained appaloosa filly with a bloodline going back to Man O' War. And she was a pistol! In March 1984 I bought my first property, in Crawford County. It was a trailer with only 2½ acres, but it was home. There I built up a rock wall surrounding the trailer base to block the wind, and a stall for the horse. The stall was not plumb, square, or level...but the horse didn't care.

This property was close to the proposed Meramec Dam Project. Hundreds of acres had been bought and left vacant while conservationists argued with the government over dam construction. Farms were abandoned, and fences deteriorated. This was an open invitation to this woman [me] with a horse, a dog, and a compass. Deer trails and abandoned roads leading to the spring-fed Meramec River and beyond beckoned. From my trailer I could ride for hours and see no one. We could swim or wade across the river and ride the wild bluffs overlooking the Meramec River. It was a freedom beyond anything I'd ever experienced. My dog, Rusty, was just as wild as the country. She was big, red, with yellow eyes. She could talk a squirrel out of a tree and have it for a snack. She was smart and my constant companion everywhere.

Wanting better grazing, in June 1985 I bought 10 acres fenced with a bit of pasture, lots of woods, and a spring-fed pond, great for fishing and skinny dipping. It also had a chicken house and a storage building. I soon acquired what people call fighting cocks, but they are beautiful, intelligent, tough chickens. There was a brief fight in spring when I let the chickens out of the henhouse. The rooster which had over-wintered outside with some hens (it wasn't my idea!) considered the area his territory. The inside rooster chose flight, and took refuge in my breezeway behind the couch. A couple hours later he ventured out and all was well, no doubt which was the boss bird.

I was decent with a chainsaw. I sharpened the blades by hand with a file and cut and split my winter supply of firewood. I used my wood stove exclusively. After I cut a tree, the horse dragged it out to the open. She was a big horse, part thoroughbred, but all appaloosa. (She is over 30 years old now and still living with friends in Stanton, MO.)

Can a city girl effectively manage a farm house in the country? Of course! I did get help with electrical problems and when lightning struck the well. And I had a friend knock a hole in the wall of my Sullivan concrete block house for a door. I got tired of carrying firewood through the house to the wood stove. A door and porch made for much less work.

I could climb up on the chicken house with aluminum paint to stop the leaks. Yes I had m.s., but it was in the early stages. I could climb to the house roof to clean the gutters and scrape the chimney. With a garage attached lengthwise, and a breezeway, there were a lot of gutters and oak trees!

I bought a horse trailer so I (we) could still escape to wild country. I made good friends because of her and explored more back country. I miss those very wonderful friends in the saddle club. Had I been able to look into the future, I never would have left. But I did explore considerably more country. And that was good.

My job transfer caused me, Rusty and Immy (nickname for Snow Image, the horse) and the chickens to move to St. Joseph where I bought a few acres in Easton, Missouri in June, 1988. I met some good neighbors for riding, and began exploring. But things fell apart on the job. Early 1990 I moved back to Franklin County, but never owned a farm again and never really recovered.

But I couldn't cut through old osage orange fence posts with a hand saw. I couldn't make the bad old days in St. Joseph go away. And I couldn't make the multiple sclerosis go away. I believe, though, I am stronger for the experience.

I love wild country. For a year I had rented a trailer with land south of Leasburg where early one morning I heard a scream that could only have been the reputedly resident mountain lion. Wow! I wrote this song there:

COUNTRY MELODY

Fire in the mountains, water in the draw,
Grandpa's chasin' my old Grandma.
Sun is settin' and evenin's nigh
Scooter's gone chasin' a firefly.

Night is comin' and the earth is still,
Pa's on the mountain by the old corn still.
Ma's in the kitchen bakin' up some bread,
Holler'n at Scooter to go off to bed.
Chorus
Country livin' I like it, it's swell
Haulin' up water from the deep cold well.
God's in Heaven all's right with me,
S'long as there's biscuits and a honeybee tree.

Stars are shinin' but there ain't no moon.
Pickin' on my guitar, workin' out a tune.
Cricket's callin' to his lady love,
Bats are circlin' in the sky above.

Coyote calling near the Hatfield barn,
Likely they'll be singin' in the early morn.
Hound dogs barkin' up an old coon tree,
Cryin' in the nursery from the new baby.
Chorus
Country livin' I like it, it's fine
Sweatin' at the sawmill, freezin' in the mine.
God's in Heaven, all's right with me,
S'long as there's fish-in' and a climbin' tree
CHARLOTTE E. SCHNEIDER   1982

PART 2

End of Forestry

CHAPTER 9

A Hand on My Heart

I CAN'T REMEMBER EXACTLY WHEN THIS happened, maybe 1982 or early '83, but I remember where. I had been working as an assistant resource forester for a few years, thoroughly enjoying the experience, ticks, fires, and all. Each year the university I graduated from with a B.S. in forest management holds a graduate day to bring graduates together and update them. So I made a hotel reservation and drove to Columbia in my trusty old green pickup truck looking forward to seeing old friends.

I met up with fellow forestry graduates and teachers. One of the teachers had a gathering planned for the evening and we were invited. Representatives from my employer were also invited and present. I was a relatively new employee within the department, but I knew several people in the hierarchy from meetings and training sessions. 'Jack Strap' (name altered), who was very high in the forestry hierarchy was there. I had a great deal of respect for this person and his experience, and his position, but that was changed abruptly.

Visiting and relaxing at the teacher's home after a long day several of us were gathered around a coffee table, probably discussing trees. Over time the others drifted off and I was sitting alone talking to 'Mr. Strap'. And then he reached across the table with his hand open and put his hand on my breast.

Time stopped. Shocked, I asked him to take his hand away. Without thinking, I remember getting up, talked to no one, found my coat and left. Walking out in the cold air helped, though I was still not thinking. Everything seemed automatic. I remember the grass crunching as I walked to my truck. Everything seemed so quiet except for the grass

51

and my breathing. I unlocked my truck got in and sat there. I knew it was cold, I could see my breath. I started the engine and sat there just staring at the window. The window was frosted. I waited. I wanted to cry and scream but couldn't. I felt my world tumbling down around me. I had sacrificed so much and worked and studied so hard to be a forester. I knew if I said anything to anyone I would lose forestry. Here it is some 30 years later and I can still feel the cold and hear the grass crunch. And I still can't cry. I feel empty.

As my truck window cleared I knew I would have to begin thinking in order to drive and find my way back to the hotel. I wasn't ready. Then my truck seemed to warm. I had the sense of a presence next to me. I didn't turn my head, I didn't need to. I felt Jesus was there with me. I let up on the clutch, gave it gas, and started off. I remember driving across town to the hotel, getting undressed, and going to bed.

Nothing had prepared me for this; not ten years as a secretary; not happy hours at the local pub; not years of dating a plethora of fellows; not a variety of supervisors; not 3½ years as one of the first and few girls in forestry school ('74-'77). I was always treated with respect. I could not make myself tell anyone what happened, I was so embarrassed. It couldn't have really happened. I thought that if I said anything, it would be blamed on me, that is what society does to women. I would lose the new career I had sought so hard, and changed my life for.

Then it happened again, to a young woman forester. But she had the courage to complain. Apparently 'Mr. Strap' had a reputation. I heard he had previously molested a secretary or two. Word moved slowly those days. The young forester left the department. I never had the courage to call her or ask about her and apologize for not warning her. I pray she did not leave forestry. Forestry does not deserve that loss. The forests are well worth extraordinary risk and sacrifice. Based on my experience some men in the hierarchy cannot be trusted.

Guilt haunted me for years. After it happened to the other woman forester I felt like I was responsible for not speaking out. If only I had told people. I then told my immediate supervisor, but I don't recall his comment. Years later the Stress Center at St. Mary's Hospital helped me deal with this experience. Some time later I tried to tell my mother what happened. She had just the reaction I expected in our society at that time. "What did you do to cause him to do that?" she asked. I pray society has changed its attitude.

It took me some time to understand what happened. Maybe it wasn't a sex thing. I'd heard this sort of experience is likely a control issue. I can believe that. He owned me. It wasn't just my career, I had given my life to forestry. But this action against me, and my lack of action in defense of my body, became like a cancer that corrupted me and began a "spiral of decline" as certain as any infection in a tree. By not fighting it, I lost whatever control I had. My defenses were severely compromised.

*"...This is the way the world ends,
Not with a bang, but a whimper."*
T.S. Eliot, "The Hollow Men"

CHAPTER 10

Death of a Dream

In June 1988, I had transferred to St. Joseph District thinking the work would be somewhat less demanding without the 24-hour call for fire fighting. I bought a small farm east of St. Joseph and had settled in with my animal family. It seemed unusual that 'Mr. Brownstone' from the Jefferson City hierarchy of the forestry division, would come to my first evaluation on the St. Joseph Forest District. But never in my worst nightmare would I have imagined what was about to happen. On February 2, 1989, I was put on probation.

In my previous position on Meramec Forest District, I had always received excellent reviews, for 10 years. Here it appeared I did nothing right. In my evaluation I was severely faulted for not learning things I had not had the opportunity to learn in Sullivan. I was trying to learn from a manual, but I guess I didn't learn from this manual fast enough.

I was even accused of discrimination based on an article from one of my landowner contacts. I placed it in the file. This landowner was an officer and editor for the local MENSA. The word *Mensa* means table in Latin. The name stands for a round-table society, where race, color, creed, national origin, age, politics, educational or social background are irrelevant. I thought of MENSA as a social group of the super high IQ people. He had written against discrimination, though the title was purposely inflammatory. Was it wrong to put this paper from my landowner in my landowner files?

But the worst was faulting me for adjusting work schedules to avoid the heat of summer afternoons outside because of my health issues. 'Mr. Brownstone' made it quite clear that I "have no business being a forester when (I) cannot function as a normal forester." This was the worst year of my life.

I tried fighting this probation on my own by filing a grievance, which was the proper procedure. I prepared documentation, which I still have, and even had an attorney in Kansas City look over my paperwork. Then after some months the attorney admitted he had been previously hired by the department. Following proper grievance procedures ended when my depression advanced far enough to be life threatening. After a futile meeting in Jefferson City, I drove to St. Louis, to my parents and home. But my parents didn't know what to do with me. I had them call friends in Sullivan, Bob and Linda, who came to St. Louis. They took me to St. Mary's Hospital Stress Center where I remained for over a month, from the middle of May to June, 1989.

The Stress Center helped me. The doctors required several months off work for me to recover strength before allowing me to return to work. After I returned, I found the district forester who had brought the allegations of poor performance against me had been promoted to a position out of Missouri. In turn the department had promoted their first woman as district forester to replace him. I felt drained and could not fight the probation any longer and don't remember discussing it with her.

During my final months I was able to put closure on a couple problems at Bluffwoods State Forest. The picnic area in Bluffwoods State Forest had a history of being vandalized. I had been told there were satanic rituals being held there. Judging by the disgusting things I had seen painted on the bathroom walls, I was not surprised. Not just that, all the metal braziers were severely broken down as if burnt from intense fires. I had been alarmed and had made efforts to stop this abusive use of a state picnic area. Also the many bridges on the trail above the site had boards missing and damage perhaps for firewood, as well as by flood waters in the steep ravines. I had taken pictures of the damaged bridges and used them in my grievance document fighting the probation. When I returned to work, I found the bridges were being repaired and made safe, and new braziers were ordered.

Also I was able to complete checking boundary line marks at Bluffwoods State Forest. Some areas were so steep I had to get to the boundary line from a ridge, then I would tuck my pants into my socks and boots and slide down on my butt. One time I pushed a snake down with me in the debris. Neither the snake nor I stuck around for introductions. The woods were beautiful. And then it was over. I miss the beauty of the ever-changing forest.

During the ten years, 1978-1988, I had worked as assistant resource forester on Meramec Forest District, I had nominated 10 dedicated forest landowners as Tree Farmers (as well as several pioneer tree farmers who were good prospects). Being a tree farmer requires foresters to inspect their land every ten years to update improvements to their timber. The landowner is expected to make improvements to their forest resource as appropriate. On 2/23/1989 I was awarded the bronze hard hat.

I include here a picture of me holding the Bronze Hard Hat awarded me for my work in Sullivan promoting forestry. I didn't appear for the awards presentation; continual crying doesn't do much for the eyes and face. Some time later in 1989 a friend and fellow forester took my picture, and here it is. I was very proud of this. I had been active on the Tree Farm committee for years. The chairman of our eastern committee, Bill Kickbush, wrote a beautiful letter commending my work which I had used in my grievance document fighting the probation.

"It's impossible to predict how long it will take a broken heart to heal. I was blessed though:With God's help..."

IMMACULEE ILIBAGIZA Left To Tell.

She suffered so much more than I during the ethnic cleansing in her country that she and her family experienced. Yet I have learned as she did, how to come closer to God through suffering.

"Hold fast to dreams, for if dreams die, life is a broken-winged bird that cannot fly."
LANGSTON HUGHES

"I do the best I know how, the very best I can; and I mean to keep on doing it to the end. If the end brings me out all right, what is said against me will not amount to anything, if the end brings me out all wrong, ten angels swearing I was right would make no difference."
ABRAHAM LINCOLN

"The greatest oak was once a little nut who held its ground."
BUDDHIST PROVERB

CHAPTER 11

Life After Forestry

AFTER TEN PLUS YEARS WORKING as a forester every day in the woods, a major demotion is hard to take. Quitting was not an option. Getting reasonable insurance, getting insurance at all, was not likely. The transfer put me working as an assistant naturalist out of Rockwoods Reservation, a forest reserve just west of St. Louis, 2/1990 to 10/1993. At least I had trees to talk to.

I had no office, no window, and no phone. My being there probably was not thrilling for the staff, I didn't notice a welcome mat put out for me. But it certainly could have been worse. A storage closet was converted as a work space for me. A drawing table became my would-be desk. I was still functioning pretty well physically when I came there, but understandably I was dealing with depression. And being inside with only moderate physical exercise was disastrous for my body. That was my work space for 3½ years.

I still had two horses and my dog. From a friend I rented a house, pasture, and barn space south of Grey Summit, and cared for his three horses and my two, though I sold him the second one I had picked up in St. Joseph. I had dated his son for some time before I left Sullivan. Though his son was gone, his son's buckskin gelding was there, so I felt like I had a friend there. My friend who owned the farm lived in Sullivan.

I still had my new 4-wheel drive red pickup truck I had bought for pulling my horse trailer. Every day while driving to work I prayed I would die in an automobile accident. No such luck. I guess it wasn't my time. Riding the horse was still good, though I don't remember going camping with the horse much anymore. I tried selling real estate, but I wasted a lot of time and energy on something I had no heart for. I sent out job applications for a sales position to numerous places and enjoyed dressing up and interviewing. But I always told them I had primary progressive multiple sclerosis and probably didn't give a strong impression, for I certainly didn't feel strong.

At work I washed bird defecation off benches every day and filled bird feeders. I fed mice to snakes and cleaned up after them. But the snakes were interesting and didn't bite me very often; and were more trustworthy than my employer. We also had a very fat salamander I fed worms to. Its defecation didn't smell nearly so bad, but it wasn't pretty. I also spent a lot of time pulling weeds in the garden, and it was always hot! I had time doing litter pickup along the trails.

I liked preparing educational displays and doing scout programs. I did enjoy doing the programs for kids. You must hold their interest with a presentation or you lose your audience. Audience feedback was great and very stimulating. I searched out Toastmasters for public speaking and did also present programs on forestry for the public.

The fellas who worked outside at Powder Valley would stop and visit briefly. That was nice. They had woodsy smells. It isn't that the entry level assistant naturalist work is bad, it isn't. It's just that after forestry, it couldn't compare. I missed working in the woods, and being part of something larger than life.

*What a man finally becomes is a composite of
all the horizons he has explored.*
SIGURD OLSON

CHAPTER 12

A New Beginning, Arboriculture

THREE AND A HALF YEARS after the demotion taking me away from forestry, I returned to forestry--October, 1993. The St. Louis District, which had taken me in as an assistant naturalist after my demotion, offered me an opportunity to work in urban forestry. Field work was not part of it. My body had deteriorated considerably in the last few years, but taking calls about trees, diagnosing problems, and prescribing treatments was a fresh opportunity to learn and grow.

I enrolled at Meramec Community College for training on shrub identification and insect and disease diagnosis. There I joined Gateway Horticultural Association (GPHA) and met several very knowledgeable horticulturists. Attending St. Louis Arborist Association (SLAA) meetings I met wonderful arborists. The department paid for me to attend an annual Midwestern Chapter conference of the International Society of Arboriculture (ISA) where I met other professional arborists. I kept challenging my knowledge with conferences and training sessions that I could afford, and could take time off for. It was very stimulating and enriching.

At the arborists association meetings, I met Bill, one of the members, so dedicated to good tree care that he was willing to lose clients rather than damage trees at a homeowner's request. Though we rarely spoke, I recognized his passion for trees. His friends and many others were equally dedicated to trees. I knew Bruce for decades as a forester and he found a good home professionally in arboriculture as a consultant as well as in the woods. And there were many others equally dedicated, but less vocal arborists. However, many good arborists had chosen to abandon the St. Louis Arborist Association rather than change it from within. Though topping (heading, tipping, rounding over, etc), flush cut pruning, over-fertilization, and other practices detrimental to trees still exist in some form, among knowledgeable arborists they are disappearing. Hopefully tree owners will stop demanding damaging practices.

Though I personally was too shy to be very vocal, I did become a Certified Arborist May 2, 1995, just 4 years after the program was begun in 1991 by the International Society of Arboriculture (217.355.1212). Also, I was the first in the department to become certified.

Certification is an excellent way to begin judging the knowledge and qualifications of individuals available to make judgments and work on public and private trees. I began administering the 4½ -hour Certified Arborist exam quarterly and taught a chapter of the Study Guide monthly for a few years. I believe in this way I was able to make a difference in St. Louis and the Midwest. People even came to take the exam from Arkansas and other neighboring states.

The International Society of Arboriculture (ISA), through their scientifically researched *Journal of Arboriculture* (name changed) and their *Arborist News* Magazine, has vastly improved arboriculture. At the same time Alex Shigo, publishing through the National Arborist Association's (NAA) *Tree Care Industry* magazine, has vastly improved pruning techniques and the understanding of tree systems. I am so grateful I had the opportunity to hear speakers like Prof. Al Shigo, Dr. Kim Coder, Dr. Thomas Smiley, Dr. John Ball, Dr. Nelda Matheny, and so very many others. Before ISA's annual International conferences they had training sessions available. I particularly remember attending a 2-day session near Kent OH by Davey Tree. Another opportunity I took advantage of was a Train-the-Trainer Hazard Tree Diagnosis session in Minneapolis MN that I drove to.

Immediately before ISA's annual conference, they hold an International Tree Climbing Competition which brings in climbers from all over the world. I was intrigued by the climbing and working-in-the-tree techniques of good climbers such as footlocking, limb walking and throw-line. Iimages and videos are available on the web. Also there is a video available on the competition held in St. Louis called At Home In a Tree. In 1995 I drove to Hilton Head Island, South Carolina, for the annual conference and there witnessed the annual International Tree Climbing Competition, observing the best of the best clearly in some immense live oak trees.

In the forest we worked with groups of trees. Quality, quantity, species, and where they are located such as north slope, south slope, east or west, is dictated by available sunlight and soil. Heat affects moisture and evaporation. Competition impacts shape of the crown, and thus ability to maximize leaf production and growth. The tree's ability to defend itself against insects and diseases depends on its ability to extract needed chemicals from the soil for nutrition and defense, as well as water for all life's activities, most notably evapo-transpiration. But of course, there are many new diseases and insects that have been imported and invaded our natural forest. Our trees' natural defenses against these are not developed.

In our natural forest environment, there are many natural enemies of tree pests. Numerous natural enemies like hover flies, and lacewings, and, yes, ladybug beetles. But now the emerald ash borer and others threaten our urban and natural forests. Can our trees develop natural enemies fast enough to save our trees? Can scientists locate local and/or imported enemies to help? The struggle against diseases is internal in the trees but probably more fascinating, albeit less colorful. Science is just scratching the surface in discovering defense chemicals that trees have been manufacturing for millions of years.

Though I am most familiar with the temperate hardwood forest of Missouri, and most intimately with that of the Ozark foothills and river hills west of St Louis and south of the glaciated plains, similarities to other forests are undeniable. While fighting fires in Southern California, New Mexico and Idaho the differences on northeast and southwest slopes is recognizable. And yes, Missouri has bears and mountain lions also.

OK, so what does this all have to do with arboriculture? Everything! I understand how swamp and wetland trees can survive on urban soils, they have evolved an ability to survive with minimum oxygen available to their roots on compacted clay soils in St. Louis. I can understand why many northern tree species can't tolerate St. Louis' hot summers, which explains why white birch seems to survive only for awhile, but by the time they get to looking like trees, they die from beetle attacks. Live oaks are beautiful trees, but when it comes to St. Louis' winters they get cold feet.

It's wonderful that dawn redwood from China can grace our city, and others like weeping katsura can decorate our homes, and it may be a distant Asian relative can save our nearly extinct but beautiful Franklin tree through an inter-generic cross. But we could do without Asian bush honeysuckle. And our elms would have been better off without the disease we call Dutch Elm Disease.

In the urban forest we still have to deal with available sunlight and water, but our buildings and watering systems change things. Buildings shade and block growth of trees' roots. Construction materials can change soil pH. Watering system installation often cuts roots. Excessive water may land on sensitive parts of roots such as the root collar, and likely watering will increase soil pH. Nutrition is seriously affected by our fertilizers, particularly where high nitrogen fertilizers with broadcast herbicides are applied to our lawn. Utility companies may tunnel under driveways when installing lines, but cut through roots on trees. And people wonder why 5-10 years or so later trees die.

Forest trees deal with floods and fires, but our urban trees also deal with lawnmowers and string trimmers, and utility companies. Just because we want a tree in a certain location doesn't mean the tree can adapt to the growing conditions. We plant trees too deep, forcing roots to survive in oxygen-starved dirt. We plant in a bowl hole from which roots often cannot escape. We let people hack at our trees' branches instead of hiring knowledgeable arborists to prune them. It is no wonder at all that trees become a hazard and fall on our house or car.

Wanting to continue sharing what I have learned about these mysterious trees isn't enough. After retirement I bought a projector and scanned thousands of tree pictures. I continued to publish my newsletter, *The Urban Tree* (in 2009 the 10th year), and through research and volunteering at the Missouri Botanical Garden Plant Doctor desk I had expanded my knowledge of the urban forest community. Of course, not driving any longer has interfered with that.

Trees have so much to teach us. In the past I was walking with physical assistance, but it has become extraordinarily difficult to move about. My energy level after dealing with the multiple sclerosis all day and night is low. On this day, August 15, 2009, I can only hope to get shrubs and trees planted for the butterflies at my home site before they haul me off to the nursing home. But I still have this moment in time.

PART 3

Life Before Forestry

"Aerodynamically, the bumblebee shouldn't be able to fly, but the bumblebee doesn't know it so it goes on flying anyway."
MARY KAY ASH

CHAPTER 13

A Brief Biography

A S A SECRETARY, I NEVER dreamed I would break into a career that would introduce me to such beauty. Being one of the first women to do this didn't scare me. I seemed to feel at home in the woods, yet there is much that needs to be shared. And healing, with God's help, will be complete.

My life originally was very ordinary. I graduated in 1964 from what was a small Catholic girl's high school in St. Louis City--Cor Jesu Academy. After gradation, I worked as a secretary for 10 years. I had joined the Sierra Club and met some very interesting and assertive people. Some of them were even women! They had goals, and an education. I learned much from them about the natural world. More important, they taught me about passion, a passion to improve the world we live in, and the importance of a quest. They taught me how to backpack and canoe. A friend taught me in detail how to use a topographic map with a compass. With these tools I developed a drive to explore, and to excel and challenge myself, and others.

I didn't intend to break any barriers in college, it just sort of happened. Forestry was, and perhaps always will be, a non-typical career for women. But Affirmative Action opened the door for me. In 1973 the University of Missouri had to make changes to accommodate women, in their forestry program, and in the fall of 1974 I was one of them. Men far outnumbered women in school. It might have been fun, but the young men were 10 years my junior, and recent high school graduates.

Forestry school seemed so very natural for me that I never considered others may not feel the same way. Hiking boots are so much more comfortable than high heels. It felt good to cram school books into a backpack, instead of lipstick into a handbag. A bicycle is a lot cheaper than a car, and easier to park.

School was wonderful. I worked hard and even became vice president of the honorary forestry fraternity, *Xi Sigma Pi*, and graduated *cum laude*—Remarkable feats for me. Forestry is a science, complete with physics, chemistry, statistics, and various math courses. This was a considerable challenge for a person not blessed with an understanding of math, but I learned.

The summer of '77 I worked in Southern California with a crew on a four-wheel drive fire truck on the Angeles National Forest. My supervisor seemed imperturbable, no matter how threatening the fire. He was inspiring and I learned valuable lessons about fire fighting. I remember riding to one fire along a steep mountain trail not wide enough for our 4-wheel drive fire truck. Sometimes only 3 wheels were on the ground. There was a fire to be put out and calculated risks were necessary to get there. He knew his equipment well.

In December of 1977, I graduated from the School of Forestry, Fisheries and Wildlife with a Bachelor of Science in Forest Management. After graduation, in January 1978, I started my career at the Little Rock Parks and Recreation. It was wonderful. I came to know all the wild areas in Little Rock and drew up an expansion plan for parks and a bikeway plan. Julius Breckling was a very inspiring supervisor. I worked there almost a year, but then received a call offering me a position in my home state, Missouri, as a forester. It was very sad leaving Little Rock, but I thought I was going on to a great forestry career, fulfilling my dream. I said goodbye and moved to Sullivan, Missouri.

Starting in November of 1978, I worked for the Conservation Department on the Meramec Forest District and for ten years totally immersed myself in forestry. They were ten incredibly fulfilling, enriching years learning to know the Missouri forests intimately. Though I was unable to secure a promotion, all was forgotten when I stepped out of the truck and into the woods.

In 1983, I was diagnosed with multiple sclerosis. Later it was determined to be primary progressive.

After ten years, the m.s. forced me to make a change. In June of 1988 I transferred to St. Joseph, Missouri, and there I was put on probation and removed from forestry. I was demoted and transferred to the St. Louis Forest District in February 1990 as an assistant naturalist. Three and a half long years later, October 1993, I was promoted back into forestry, urban forestry, where I became an arborist, and then a Certified Arborist. I certainly recommend employing qualified Certified Arborists for any tree work around your home.

Eight years later I retired. Time and energy allowed volunteering at the Missouri Botanical Garden, as a Plant Doctor for 7 years until the summer of 2009. No longer able to drive my conversion van has complicated being able to volunteer. Moving into my rebuilt family home, I now have the opportunity to practice what I have been preaching and am establishing my own arboretum on this relatively small—approximately 6750 sq.ft.—urban lot. I continued to publish *The Urban Tree* newsletter, but in the 10th year, my energy is running out.

In the process of healing I have been writing and rewriting this autobiography for 19 years, since 1989. It is appropriate to put closure on it in the 20th year. However, as one door closes, two windows are opening. I am starting three other books. One I started yesterday on my other computer: Bending the Rules, explaining my struggles with advanced chronic progressive multiple sclerosis. The other Trees in my Mind, is an expansion of the section on "Remembering" and "life principles I have learned from trees", and Diary of an Urban Arboretum. Will I finish them? I don't know. Will I make it through even this 24-hour period?

"I Will Never Leave You or Forsake You."
GOD
Hebrews 13.5

CHAPTER 14

Reminiscing

IT HAS BEEN SO LONG, I have almost forgotten the comfort a campfire can provide–the crackle of the burning wood, and aroma of the smoke. I love to hear the wind blow through the trees. Occasionally you would hear sounds in the forest at night as animals go out on their rounds, or trees bend and crack to their swaying. As a transplanted single woman doing a man's job in a small town of 6000 people, I got to spend a lot of time by myself

My first year living and working in the country, 1979, I tamed this big red dog which had been a castoff along the road where I rented a trailor. She was pretty uncivilized and I had to keep the door open that winter so she could dash out when the furnace went on. But eventually she got used to me and the furnace. We were together for over ten years. We hunted and fished together. She could 'talk' a squirrel out of a tree with her yellow eyes. I saw her twice enjoy her squirrel snack.

We camped together, and I never felt threatened despite being far from civilization. I often went camping alone. My idea of camping was pretty primitive; all I needed was a spot to throw my sleeping bag, and maybe build a campfire. Though Rusty chased an occasional something, she never strayed far. She was my constant companion.

After I learned about the MS in 1983, I felt it was time to buy land and a horse. In 1984, I bought 2 acres and a trailer in Crawford County south of Sullivan. And the three of us–me, rusty and Immy (my new 2-year old appaloosa filly)-- spent a lot of time together, which included camping. In 1985, I bought 10 acres so we had more room and my family grew to include chickens. I met some very wonderful friends, Bob and Linda Bach, and their son Kevin.They sort of took me 'under their wing' and guided me to a better understanding of life with a young horse just barely green-broke by a local horse trainer.

I found companions and adventure at rendezvous—a combination of primitive camping and competitive black powder target shooting. I built many friendships. My dog was always welcome at the camps. She respected other people's campsites and never caused a problem. Before the camp awoke, we took long walks. She must have been imposing enough, because no one bothered us, and I often slept out away from camp.

It certainly was different from the life I had lived as a single woman in St. Louis--partying, indulging in Friday-night happy hours and too many cocktails. In Sullivan, I might go to a bar and have a drink but did not know anyone there, so I wrote. I guess a single girl alone at a bar was unheard of. Two drinks and it was time to go home, alone, before I fell asleep.

The one thing missing in my life was a man to camp and travel with. Sunrises and sunsets should be shared. The wooded hillsides bathed in sunlight are beyond description. The smells of fresh wildflowers and musty, moist woodlands still linger in my mind. I have tasted icy frost flowers and fresh mushrooms. Ripe blackberries, and raspberries, blueberries on dry slopes, and gooseberries in open woodlands, were always a welcome treat.

Making friends to ride with was wonderful. But even with friends, they were still lonely years. But the dog and the horse, the farm and the chickens, the firewood splitting and cutting, the gutter cleaning, chimney repair and cleaning, and the myriad other tasks of a farm owner, kept me busy enough. An occasional visitor from out of the area helped me to remember what I was missing. And life goes on. If I had it to do all over again, I really would change very little...mostly my attitude and expectations.

"Lord Grant Me the Serenity to Accept the Things I Cannot Change, the Courage to Change the Things I Can, and the Wisdom to Know the Difference."
SAINT FRANCIS OF ASSISSI

CHAPTER 15

Childhood Memories

WHEN DO WE QUIT BLAMING everyone and everything else for our problems and take responsibility for our own lives? There are many things about myself I cannot change. Past experiences and feelings woven together are an integral part of my person. These help me determine how I will act and react to today's challenges.

There is no doubt when I was born what position I was destined to play, what level of the family hierarchy I would typically achieve. A girl in a German Catholic family hopes to marry well and fulfill the position of wife and mother. On my own I tried to rise above the position I was born into, and found it difficult. Lack of self-esteem carried over into my career. I could not create the self respect and self esteem needed to function boldly, and found myself preyed upon by people who were secure. It is said whatever you believe to be true your subconscious will make certain it comes to pass. So I victimized myself.

Why would a girl need to go to college? Girls should be ladies and mothers. Girls play with dolls, not trucks. Men play on teams where they learn to compete and cooperate. I learned how to keep the house clean, and serve others. At home I did not watch the news because women belonged in the kitchen to clean dishes after meals so the men could relax in the living room and keep up with the news. The house, and particularly the kitchen, was mom's territory.

Faces in my past left impressions I used to mold my personality. Parents and family, friends and acquaintances, teachers at school, the bible and my Catholic education, and of course that new media- -television, seemed to encourage a woman's role in the home. We say and do things that cause us to receive feedback often in the form of body language, visual signals like a finger to the lips for silence. Better not chew gum.

We don't always interpret signals correctly. Senders may use inaccurate signals, sometimes with bad intentions. If our experience and knowledge are based on inaccurate information, confusion increases. It seems life is a continual seeking after accuracy, the truth.

As children we receive lots of negative messages. Early childhood is a time of intense learning. Many thoughts, ideas, and questions, require a response from adults. Adults are often stressed by too much to do and too little time, money, desire, knowledge, or understanding. Mature adults can take this into account when we receive the response. But a child often misinterprets. We must be careful of the messages we send and constantly check to see that our messages are being received accurately.

Parents, teachers, ministers have a responsibility to build strong minds and bodies. Say positive things to your children, your friends, your acquaintances. Everyone cannot be president of the United States, but everyone has the right to reach their full potential and to carve out a nitch for themselves. Build a child's self confidence and self esteem, don't tear it down. And bless them.

I am not a child anymore. I am responsible for my life. I really can't complain about the way I was raised. Both my parents, German immigrants who met here in St. Louis, and married, raising 3 kids, infused a sense of adventure just by who they were and their ability to survive and thrive. They had to be risk takers to make that transition. They taught me to respect people. They taught me to have a healthy respect for resources such as money. They gave me a good, safe, clean home and education.

"As the twig is bent so grows the tree."
AUTHOR UNKNOWN

CHAPTER 16

Beyond Childhood

I FIND MYSELF STILL REBELLING. WHAT happened to cause my innate insecurity? gender casting? Women were/are cast into diminutive roles. Women, like men, need to develop to the full extent of our capabilities, not be framed to fit a particular mold. An ability, or desire, or willingness to do things not considered "womanly" should not tag a person as an aberrant to society. Sociological mores have a long way to go in maturing. Long before there was a "take-our-daughter-to-work day, girls were routinely taught that being too capable, too smart, or too ambitious would make them unfeminine, unlovable, and unmarried. The primal fear of abandonment, of success as a roadway to loneliness, can hit a woman hard. Obliged to choose between success at work or fulfillment after hours socially, many women consciously or unconsciously choose the later. The "liberation" of women has opened doors, but the floor is very slippery, and the proverbial ceiling made of concrete not glass. How long will we surrender our lives to "what if" and simply "do".

What did this have to do with me? Everything! I tried the normal route. But ten years as a secretary led me to consider other alternatives. I wasn't married and seemed to be dodging prospects. And when a friend I'd met through the Sierra Club suggested going to college, I couldn't think of a reason not to, so I did. He never expected I would be one of the first women to study forestry in Missouri. The school had just opened forestry to women in 1973. Wow! And I graduated 3½ years later; I had a year's worth of credits from night school.

Enter the woman into the male-dominated career of forestry. Based on personal research I was one of the first ten women in state forestry in America. I am not and never could be, one of the "good old boys," though I tried. I never learned how to hunt or fish well, but it was a great excuse to be in the woods. I am responsible for my decisions, good and bad. Past experience helps me determine my future. And I pray. I forgive others for what they could have done to help me and did not do. I forgive myself for what I could have done to help myself, and did not. There are no limits to what I can accomplish with God's help. And there is no time like the present to begin. The route may change, but the hoped-for destination is the same as ever.

When we make decisions we need to rise above past feelings and experiences. A lifetime of experiences gives us new perspectives. It takes a lifetime to determine the depth of the effect on our lives. Had we chosen the "other road" would our lives really be so much better?

I think it is the little decisions that really have the impact on our lives and others. The decision to call a friend not seen for awhile; the kind, or hurtful, words said to an unknown person in a restaurant; the chance to help someone not taken. These are the little decisions that impact lives, that fill us with love or hate. These are the decisions that bring us closer to joy, to God, to our faith, or take us down a path of isolation and despair. And in the end whether it be at age 20 or 40 or 80, this is what really matters.

I set myself up for failure by not believing in myself. I was successful advising land owners on how to improve their forest, but failed to sway management on my administrative abilities. I failed to communicate. I failed to develop the tools to succeed in forestry regardless of my disability. So I lost field forestry as a career.

Because I had to maintain a position at the department to maintain my insurance I gradually moved closer to St. Louis. July 1 1997 my older brother Richard died; he was only 57. It is sad to see elderly parents lose a favored son. They had been very close and depended on him. In a few short months advanced prostrate cancer moved throughout his body, and our lives were changed forever. Eleven months later, less than a year, my father died. What is really important in life?

Just before my brother died I had begun attending a Catholic Charismatic service. God must have been preparing me for this coming loss. There is no describing the difference prayer has made in my life. As a forester I had felt close to God, working every day in the forest, seeing up close the magnificence of his creation. But it could never possibly compare with the closeness and love I feel through the many prayers, the love, the understanding, the excitement, the beneficence of Jesus. God is the reason we are here. His hand touches all parts of our lives. He is there to guide us and protect us. Though He allows us to make our own decisions, He is there to turn to for help and guidance, and love, and understanding.

At 50, I broke out of the dead career trap. I realized that there is life beyond field forestry. What happens in life is uncertain, there is no real security. Anything can happen at any time. A car crash, illness, change in personal relationships can change everything. Faith, religion, prayer, reconciliation, love, acceptance, these are secure. Failing is part of growing. I am learning to give myself permission to fail, in order to grow.

I am sad for the talents I have not developed. I am caught in a mold as surely as an insect caught in pine resin. I choose to work with things that don't care what gender I am, or whether I walk with a walker, if at all. Trees don't question; they put their whole body into each day. And they go on with life.

"I was living proof of the power of prayer and positive thinking, which really are almost the same thing. God is the source of all positive energy, and prayer is the best way to tap into His power."
IMMACULEE ILIBAGIZA

She survived ethnic cleansing in her home country and is regarded as one of the world's leading speakers on peace, faith, and forgiveness. She shares her powerful message in books and programs.

I find a great thing in this world is not so much where we stand as in what direction we are moving. We must sail sometimes with the wind and sometimes against it. But we must sail and not drift, nor lie at anchor.

OLIVER WENDELL HOLMES

CHAPTER 17

Sailing the Inland Sea

A COUPLE YEARS BEFORE RETURNING TO college I somehow met up with Mrs. Coad. She sailed a Rhodes Bantam on Carlysle Lake, Illinois, and needed a crew member for racing. Very quickly she taught me the rudiments of sailing, and how to keep the spinnaker full of maximum wind and the jib from luffing, regardless of the weather. Dedicated to sailing she spent her winters studying how she could improve. Most every weekend in summer was spent racing. The first year we consistently took third place; the second year we took 2nd. The 3rd she was taking 1st, but I was in school in Columbia, Missouri.

The Rhodes Bantam was small, about 20 feet, but carried 3 sails. When the spinnaker went up the jib came down, so I definitely had my hands full. The unused sail had to be stuffed in a bag until the mark was rounded and direction changed, all this while keeping the sails full. Wind and competition dictated fast movement. When beating into the wind, I had to quickly hang my butt over the edge and lean out to keep the boat balanced for maximum speed.

The race was set up on a triangle, so usually you had a following wind, a head on wind, and an angled wind. I have forgotten so much. With the spinnaker flying and a good wind that little boat would pick up and skim across the top of the waves so fast and so smooth, I would hear a shhhhhhhhhhhhhh sound. It was beautiful, but I had to concentrate on keeping the spinnaker full to the max, and the lines straight, and be ready to come about and move the spinnaker to the other side of the boat...the lake was not that wide!

And when we needed to round the mark, get the spinnaker in and the jib out and cut to the inside of the mark surrounded by competitors' boats as well as lots of other class racers, well, it got exciting! With a good wind it was anything but neat, and often got kind of messy, definitely dicey.

Much as I liked flying the spinnaker, beating into the wind was truly fast. The Rhodes had very little wood in the water except the foot board when racing with a good wind. With my toes under rope straps I hung out as far as possible while holding the lines for the jib to fine tune the set. The Venturi Principle, where lots of wind was forced through the narrow gap between the jib and mainsail, would really move that boat. And then shore would come up fast and we would have to tack, bringing the jib and lines around...fast! Just thinking about it gets my adrenalin going.

Once I crewed on a Flying Dutchman, but not for a race, thank God. To hang off a line from the top of the mast when beating into the wind you would stand on the side of the boat and hang on with a trapeze. What did I learn from all this? Maybe to keep my insurance paid up. When I returned to college the first elective I took was swimming!

Years later, reminiscing, I put this poem together:

Beating For Home

Sometimes when a fog settles over my mind
And my thoughts drift away to a livelier time,
I remember when a sailor friend and me
Rode the white-winged birds of the inland sea.

Raising the colors, full and high,
Our sleek little Bantam would lift with a sigh.
Now I'm rolling my easy chair to make it behave
Like the bow in a clash with a white-tipped wave.

Holding my breath as if I were there
Rounding the mark, close as we dare,
The sails are set close, the lines pulled taut,
When my white-capped skipper yells "come about!"

Feel the gush as we rush full into the wind
Then make a quick check what position we're in.
It's great to know we're first--all alone,
Last leg of the race--we're beating for home.
CHARLOTTE E. SCHNEIDER, 1985

CHAPTER 18

Impact of the Sierra Club

A ROUND 1970, I BECAME ACTIVE in the Sierra Club. I met several knowledgeable, inspiring people. Becoming active on their forestry committee I learned there was more than one way to manage a forest. There was a young forester on the committee who suggested that the impact of the attitudes the committee could encourage may be beneficial, or maybe not. The main controversy at the time was clear cutting, a form of even-aged management. But clear cutting, removing all trees from a location, is much different in California than in Missouri. Species of trees, size of area, cutting techniques, watershed, etc. all dictate the best techniques.

We need to make informed decisions. And we need to be able to change our minds and adapt. Often nature shows us the best way, though it may differ with our needs. For instance, as a forester I learned hard maple, being shade tolerant, invades our best oak-growing sites, such as many north and east slopes. Oaks have good markets, including veneer for furniture and construction. Missouri maples have only marginal markets due to reputedly inferior quality. Oaks grow acorns which feed a myriad of animals such as such as deer, turkey, ducks and geese, squirrels, and field mice. The fruits of maple are not widely used by Missouri mammals. And the controversy will rage on. Changes in management must hold up to the test of time and environmental changes.

A biologist friend I dated shared much of his skills with me, and I am eternally grateful to him. George taught me valuable lessons like how to read and understand and relate to topographic maps, and how to use a compass. This knowledge made finding my way in the woods very simple, and my comfort level in the woods very high, except for ticks and chiggers. He moved away but I carried on with the Sierra Club. I learned canoeing. For example I learned how NOT to kiss a rock on a flooded stream, and that night I learned why not to sleep in a tent which had not had the seams sealed against rain. I also learned how to backpack though I had not ventured out of Missouri except for a week on Isle Royale with the Wolf Sanctuary members. I was the only one backpacking and it was wonderful. I learned much about plant and animal identification from people dedicated to the environment.

I also met Mr. James Brewer while he was supervisor for the Mark Twain National Forest in Missouri. Through programs and activities he hosted for the forestry committee, he taught me an appreciation for the forest community. But most important, late in 1972 at an outside training session in the Paddy Creek wilderness area of the National Forest, he asked me the rhetorical question: "Why not go back to school?" I couldn't answer that question, so August of 1974, I moved to Columbia, Missouri, to study forest management at the School of Forestry, Fisheries & Wildlife, which tumbled me headlong into a most unusual career. After graduation he and his family took me on a trip to the Boundary Waters Canoe Area wilderness, a wild, wild area in Minnesota near Canada. What a fantastic trip. There are advertising videos available on the web.

Initiation into forestry school included pulling myself along a rope above a wet, muddy creek and similar activities. Wet and muddy on a frosty fall evening, we initiates were treated to hot dogs hamburgers and chips. They tasted great! I thank the Sierra Club for preparing me to get cold, wet, and muddy, and for teaching me to question management and not be afraid to stand up for the environment.

Beginning a fireline from a safe location, a 4-person crew can build and hold a lot of fireline through deep woods. This picture is courtesy of the *Sullivan Independent News*, Sullivan, Missouri.

PART 4

Recovering From Trauma

"Every man is said to have his peculiar ambition. Whether it be true or not, I can say for one that I have no other so great as that of being truly esteemed of my fellow men, by rendering myself worthy of their esteem. But if the good people in their wisdom shall see fit to keep me in the background, I have been too familiar with disappointments to be very much chagrined. Your friend and fellow citizen."

ABRAHAM LINCOLN
New Salem, March 9, 1832

CHAPTER 19

Reject Rejection

Trees do not understand failure. They are preyed upon by insects and diseases, but always they fight for their piece of the sun. How can I do less? Trees do not understand guilt or fear, depression or remorse. They do not hate or discriminate. When a part breaks off, the tree develops buds and tries to grow another limb in response to sunlight. It will continue to produce food to feed the community. All the tree knows is to keep on growing, and to keep reaching for the sun.

Neither does the tree notice if an old forester leans against it for strength or balance, or sits beneath its shade to cool off. It does not notice if a forester rolls across its roots on a scooter, or looks out of the car window to admire its strength and graceful limbs. There is room in this world for trees that are gnarled and twisted from the wind or otherwise challenged. So too there is room in this world for an old female forester with M..S.

How many times was I rejected for a promotion by my employer? Last count I remember was 13. No explanation ever was provided of why I was turned down. Abraham Lincoln speaks of humility and hope, but it's difficult. I kept thinking next time it would be different. Next time they would recognize my qualities and would promote me. As the M.S. advanced I became more concerned. Thomas Edison, the Wright Brothers, Abe Lincoln, Rosa Parks and many successful men and women did not give up in their struggles just because they failed.

It's too late to change the past. We must go on into the future with our minds and hearts open to change and opportunity. Each day is a new opportunity to grow, to learn new things, to experience new feelings. Even the great saint, Francis of Assisi, came near to being killed as a heretic by local church authorities before the Pope honored his mission. If I must choose between being humble before God, and being esteemed by my employers, I choose God.

Successful executives view failures as "false starts," "stumbles," or steps to greatness. When a poor Russian cabinetmaker's son was fired from a do-it-yourself hardware retailer, he went on to establish Home Depot. Edison, when asked how it felt to fail 1000 times replied, "I didn't fail 1000 times. The light bulb was an invention with 1001 steps." Having received his first social security check, Colonel Sanders, searching for financial security, decided to take his chicken recipe public, traveling around the country in search of a chicken restaurant to try it, and sleeping in his car. I heard it required over 1000 visits to restaurants before he found one willing to try his recipe.

We are responsible for how we react to stressors in our lives. Fill your days with good thoughts. Be proud, but be humble. My horse taught me how to fall, but on my own I learned how to get up. It doesn't matter how many times you fall, it only matters how many times you get up, and it better be the same. And you want to be quick, otherwise you get stiff and disoriented. You can always stop to catch your breath and choose a direction once you are safe from whatever threatens. Don't lay there in the road waiting to get run over like I did, be smart!

As a person, I have advantages trees do not. I can get out of the way of a bulldozer. I can eat what is healthy for me. However, being an organism, we are similar to trees. I have a disease that is preying on my body, and I will grow old, decline, and die. Unlike trees, I have a soul. Though this body will decay, my spirit will live on. Hopefully my Lord will see fit to include me in His kingdom. And I hope there will be trees and forests in heaven.

Success isn't final, failure isn't fatal, it's courage that counts.
Winston Churchill

We are what we repeatedly do. Excellence
then is not an act but a habit.
Aristotle

The only way of discovering the limits of the possible, is
to go a little way beyond them into the impossible.
ARTHUR C. CLARK

CHAPTER 20

Walking On Fire

I'M NOT SURE OF THE year, maybe it was 1992. I was trying to survive loss of my career and find a way to motivate myself and survive with the m.s. I was about 45 years old. An advertisement in a community newspaper about a fire walk attracted me, so I called and made an appointment for a Saturday evening adventure. My dog Rusty and I were camped out that night at a primitive mountain man rendezvous where I shot black powder guns in competition. I considered myself able to take care of myself, but was cautious and had cautiously prepared for this unusual focus into my inner strength.

If someone had told me I would ever do this, I would have suggested he was crazy. Rusty waited by my truck. There were several of us coming together to walk on fire. We gathered together on the porch of this rambling country house. The others seemed like normal, unthreatening people in search of an adventure, and we exchanged small talk without getting real personal. One family brought their two children. The young boy had brought his collection of stones which he seemed to believe made him strong, recognizing a power in the stones which was a bit too new age for me. But who am I to comment negatively, especially on this night. Stones are strong, God knows He created them.

We neither ate nor drank nor smoked any intoxicating anything. The history of walking on fire goes perhaps beyond recorded time, it was fascinating just to be there. For me it was learning to deal with some emotions that haunted me since I had lost forestry. The leader brought out a flip chart and started preparing us for the adventure. He introduced us to a couple young fellows who would walk beside us outside the pit, and a young woman who would lead the first walk. Then he started talking about getting around, over, and through barriers.

Though not a religious talk, he discussed recognizing the spirit and inner strength. He told the story of a small child who encountered an obstacle on the way to his favorite fishing hole and asked us what we would suggest for overcoming this obstacle. Meanwhile an immense pile of wood burned in the distance. The moon was coming up, full and bright.

Quietly we walked over to the pile of burning wood. For some time we watched it burn. As it burned down, we put paper notes of things we wanted to put behind us that we had prepared earlier. The moon was so bright it blocked out the stars. The night felt cool when we stepped away from the fire. The leader paired each of us with another individual from the group and instructed us to work as a team and imagine walking the pit as we practiced walking across the grass. I was paired with a man about my age who looked like a business man.

We were, of course, barefoot, and the grass was wet and cool. The two of us started practicing and visualizing and then would congratulate each other as we completed the imaginary walk. We practiced and congratulated each other several times on our success. We visualized walking the fire pit again and again. We always congratulated each other on our walks. And <u>then</u> it was time.

Silently, we moved to the fire pit. The wood had burned down to hot, glowing coals and the young fellows were spreading the coals. They had asked us earlier if as a group we wanted a round pit or rectangular. I requested rectangular. Though I was still walking, I didn't trust my balance. I did not want to worry about falling down in a round pit, and I wanted to know I had help close. The others agreed and the coals were spread accordingly.

And there it was, a rectangular pit filled with hot, glowing, pulsing coals. Silence prevailed as each of us was caught in our own private world. It was time to walk on fire. The young woman who had walked hot coals before started, to show how easy it was, a natural pace without fear. A few moments later she was across and the others were congratulating her with hugs.

And then someone else walked, and then another. Several had gone two or three times, but I had not yet walked, I was not yet ready.

No one pressured me; walking was an option. There was something I had to reconcile with myself before I could walk; I knew that I had to forgive myself before I could walk. I had to forgive myself for failing. And then I was ready.

The coals seemed soft, like clouds. I took another step, and another, and another, and another. I certainly never paused, but they were controlled, deliberate steps. A few more steps and the walk was complete. I was being congratulated, and the feeling was sweet. And then I turned and looked across the pit., and walked again.

I walked again, but when I was two thirds across the pit I had a weak moment, a moment of fear. The leader told us earlier that if we felt heat underfoot, we should immediately throw up our hands to the sky, throwing the heat up and out of our body, letting the heat pass through our body and up to the sky. I did just that, it was euphoric.

Then it was over, the coals were cooling. We gathered again briefly, then it was time to go back to our own lives. It was a weekend and I was camped out over at Daniel Boone's home that night along the Missouri River. It wasn't far, and it wasn't particularly late. I headed to my truck, saying good night to others I saw going to their vehicles. Rusty was waiting joyfully for my return to the truck.

As I drove I felt a blister forming on my thumb, an interesting memento of the experience. I had actually walked on fire! When I arrived back at camp buckskinners were gathered around a central fire and individual campfires. Some Native American friends were there. Friends knew where I had gone. No one was boisterous, asking more with their eyes than with words. I confirmed that I had indeed walked on fire. No one pried, and after a time, I slipped off to my own camp and curled up in my sleeping blankets.

After an event such as that walk, I'll never be the same. I overcame a demon that night. I failed as a forester and been kicked out of the woods. Before I could walk on fire, I knew I had to forgive myself for making mistakes, for being found inferior. And you know...that's o.k.

The greatest hazard in life is to risk nothing. ...Those who avoid risk may avoid suffering and sorrow, but they cannot learn, feel, change, grow, love and live...Only the person who risks can be free.
AUTHOR UNKNOWN

"Pick battles big enough to matter, small enough to win"
JONATHAN KOZOL

CHAPTER 21

Attacking Back

WHEN YOU FALL DOWN, GET up. You need to concentrate on mental, physical, and especially spiritual strength builders. You need all your faculties to get you through hard times.

SPIRITUAL EXERCISE

There is another exercise far more important, it goes beyond physical exercise. Though as a forester I had slipped away from regular worship, I had become deeply spiritual being surrounded by God's magnificent creation, and that made coming back easier. I urge you to find God in your life.

NUTRITION

You must eat foods to fuel your body. Without the needed proteins, vitamins, minerals, hormones, carbohydrates, starches, and an understanding of how your body functions, you cannot live up to your potential. Take the time to see how your body reacts to the foods you eat. Some will make you feel strong and boost your vitality. Others will drag you down and sap your energy. Your vigor depends on the genetic code you are dealt at inception. We are learning more with DNA studies, and have much more to learn. Your vitality depends on the environment you surround yourself with and the food you consume.

EXERCISE

You cannot grow strong without exercise. I strongly recommend going to a good gym and daily exercise at home. What kept me mobile so long was the hard work I did walking in the woods, and the fresh air.

At home on the farm I had horse care and riding. I had sold my farm in Sullivan and bought a farm house and 3 acres in Easton, 10 miles east of St. Joseph Missouri. More chores and plenty more exercise growing and throwing hay, but no chainsaw work cutting firewood.

Even trees exercise. The blowing in the wind exercises the branches and the trunk, and the roots. It stretches the fibers. Leaves, limbs, and trunks are made to take advantage of the least little breeze while protecting themselves from the stronger breezes by rolling leaves or shedding pieces of branches.

Exercise releases natural happy drugs which fill your system and make it possible to exercise even more, to release even more happy drugs. There of course is a limit. Mostly we set our limits too soon. Doctors can advise you, but you need to read your own body. I have found exercise very helpful in keeping my body in working order. Maybe now I have been too easy on my body and wimp out too often and too soon, but I get tired. Fatigue is a problem with MS.

After I lost forestry in 1989, I needed to find a way to have strenuous exercise, so I joined a gym. That and my horseback riding and farm life on the rented farm helped. I had continued with gym membership until my driving ceased in 2009. I have extensive gym equipment here, but my stamina is gone.

Exercise has not kept me from deteriorating, but it has made life more livable. If I did not have the outdoor exercise, hiking up and down forested hills cruising timber and fighting forest fires, instability would have come on much quicker. My sedentary lifestyle, sitting at a computer and telephone all day, contributed to my decline.

Of course, I was doing much better before my brother got sick and died July 1, 1997. A year later my father died. The stress taking care of my brother's estate in Illinois didn't help. My mother lived to be 98. She died on Palm Sunday, April 1, 2007. I had to handle her burial and estate also. I have a brother in Iowa, but we don't communicate anymore. And I have a niece and her family in Nevada who are delightful to talk to.

MENTAL EXERCISE

Volunteering at the Missouri Botanical Garden after I retired from work was a wonderful growth opportunity. To share my knowledge of trees with their knowledge of plants, and compare that with a myriad of experts, and research manuals, was extraordinarily stimulating. We need mental exercise to keep our right brain and left brain communicating. Get it somehow.

OTHER STRENGTH BUILDERS:

Friendships
Toastmasters
Social groups and societies
Volunteering
Political activism
Entrepreneural ventures
Education
Walking

"Do the thing you fear and the death of that fear is certain"
RALPH SMEDLEY, JR. founder of Toastmasters

CHAPTER 22

Toasting Toastmasters

THE TWO YEARS I WAS in St. Joseph, 1988-1989, I joined the St. Joseph Toastmasters and attended their weekly meetings. I completed my first 10 prepared speeches there qualifying me for my award as a Certified Toastmaster. Toastmasters is an international organization dedicated to improving public speaking and communication skills.

When I returned to Franklin County there wasn't a local organization, so I advertised to start one in order to continue improving my skills and find a way to present public programs in forestry. I lived farther east in Franklin County than previously, I was close to work and close to St. Louis, but still in the country.

I joined two St. Louis clubs close to my parents' home while I advertised to start a club in Franklin County. Also I became a District Officer--Vice President of Leadership and Education--for the St. Louis Area. I even received an appreciation award in 1991-2. At a time when I struggled to survive and rebuild hope, Toastmasters was there.

I didn't know how to run a Toastmasters meeting, I didn't even own a gavel or timer. But people answered my ads and the Franklin County Toastmasters was formed.. I could not have accomplished it without Phyllis, Scott, Carl, Jeff, Mark, Harry, John and others. We learned together, thank you.

Toastmasters has a long history of members helping members. The organization has been a model for many strong companies and strong leaders. You stand up, say your name, and you are applauded, I really needed that support at the time. In January 1992, I became an Able Toastmaster and also acquired an ATM bronze in May 1993, by extended speeches and starting a new club.

I have heard toastmasters give really extraordinary and sometimes emotional speeches, telling of great struggles and great successes. Sharing struggles through speeches that are timed and evaluated for organization, format and delivery by fellow members helps put life in perspective.

I remember Helen, Tom and Swan in St. Joseph who taught me that being an officer was as natural as eating. They inadvertently prepared me for my next venture in Franklin County, starting a club, and training officers. Swan taught me to put my heart and soul into a speech, and practice, practice, practice. He was a very accomplished speaker and did well in competition, the annual speech contest.

When I was returned to forestry 3½ years later, I had to move to the city. I had enough mental challenge on the job learning urban forestry/ arboriculture that I dropped Toastmasters, which meant leaving my club in Franklin County; I miss them. The club carried on the tradition of having a good time while learning, without me. Most of them came to my retirement including John Griesheimer, who was voted a Missouri Senator and brought a "Proclamation" to my retirement which was wonderful and I keep it next to my exercise equipment. I still see him on television occasionally and he looks great, as ever.

Now that I am retired it would be nice to get back to a club. Maybe I can start one in my home. Who knows what the future holds.

"Each friend represents a world in us, a world possibly not born until they arrive, and it is only by this meeting that a new world is born."
ANAIS NIN

CHAPTER 23

Friends Are Angels Too

I CANNOT MAKE IT ALONE. THROUGHOUT my life I have depended on the affirmation and confirmation of friends. More than that, they are God's representatives here on earth, they reach out with His hands and with His heart.

In forestry I worked with professional foresters and other professionals whose expertise and attention to detail was honorable and familial. But it's my dear friend Kathy who has provided continuing support. Part fire dispatcher and part administrative assistant she did her best to keep me on the straight and narrow. Though not unscathed by life experiences, we have survived and shared similar experiences and challenges growing up, and hopefully we will remain lifetime friends. Kathy also keeps me up to date on coworkers and friends in Sullivan. After 10 years there, it was home to me.

The men on the work crews I considered friends. I remember each, and the fire fighting and other field work we did together. I would have visited when they retired, but the body just did not allow these excursions. And my supervisors were friends to me also, Woody and Bob and Rich. In truth, I mostly would have gone to see the woods. So many visions move through my mind, so many memories. I haven't gone fishing or hunting or camping or called up an owl in a very, very long time.

I made friends in St. Joseph also whom I had to say goodbye to under duress. Looking back, I hope they can remember me in the early good times. Depression together with the M.S. was dreadful. Thank you for the support they tried to show me. Often I think of friends at Rockwoods, and at Powder Valley. Roseann keeps me aware of some changes. I have put much behind me, sort of compartmentalized memories, but I remember many other friends over the years, in government offices and businesses. All I can do is keep you and the many land owners, and the many trees, in my thoughts and prayers. And life goes on.

Lord make me an instrument of Thy peace. Where there is hatred, let me sow love. Where there is injury, pardon. Where there is doubt, faith. Where there is despair, hope, Where there is darkness, light. Where is sadness, joy. Oh Divine Master, grant that I may not so much seek to be consoled as to console, to be understood as to understand, to be loved as to love. For it is in giving that we receive. It is in pardoning that we are pardoned, and it is in dying that we are born to Eternal life.
St. Francis Of Assisi

Friends since forestry have been my support. Thank you to Trish and Jim who continue to rescue me. Thank you to for friends like Bob and Sonny and their family and coworkers who rebuilt my family home and reconstructed it to serve my needs in many ways. They have rescued me many times also. And others have helped me maintain the house. Marian's son David did a wonderful job tuck pointing and putting my rock wall and steps together. Marian has been a solid supporter of my prayer group when others have been called to other responsibilities. And prayer is so important.

Many volunteers at the Missouri Botanical Garden have become friends because of a sincere interest in improving our environment that we share. Their exquisite knowledge of a wide range of plants and willingness to dedicate hours to increasing their knowledge and educating others is truly admirable. Since I am not driving, I miss joining and sharing with them.

A good friend in horticulture, Justine, has given me many hours of her professional horticultural experience to help get my woods trail planted in front, and my forest island in the back, even including her son and husband. And Bob from my parish takes care of the grass, though I have not left him much, and he plants shrubs for me.

Friends like Trish and Jim, and Kathy, and Charlie, and Bob, and David and April, and so very many other angels help me put my house in order. And those like Heidi and Charlie and Bill and Kathy who deliver me to doctors or stores or wherever.

And there are old family friends, like Carl and Lucia, Heidi and Michael, Liz and Don, and new friends like Marian and her family, and Kathy and Sonny, are such a blessing. Neighbors like the Hinrichs, Edmondsons, and Berras, and Tillie and Monica were there for me. And I had two very young friends, Miles and Savannah, who have helped me and kept me thinking young. And of course my Godmother, Rose Rita, is a jewel. But the best friend I have is Jesus. Who He will send me tomorrow I don't know, but it will take many angels to keep me going. *Deo gracias, Deo gracias, Deo gracias*

"At that time there shall arise Michael, the Great Prince, guardian of your people."
The Book of Daniel 12:1

CHAPTER 24

Embracing Catholicism

I WAS BORN DECEMBER 1946 TO parents who were dedicated, responsible and loving Catholic immigrants from Germany. Beginning education was first in beautiful St. Cecelia Church and grade school where I was first touched by the Holy Spirit in Baptism. I remember as a child memorizing the Gospel of St. John just for the fun of it, it was so beautiful.

At 3rd grade we moved to Shrewsbury to be close to the seminary for my brother. We weren't a particularly religious family, just doing our duty as Catholics attending church and supporting the Catholic Kolping Society. We had a huge Bible at home with good pictures, but it was heavy and graced the bookshelf for years. There I was in St. Michael the Archangel parish and grade school. There I received Confirmation, again to the Holy Spirit. Graduation was in 1960. And that is where I am today, 30+ years later, in my family home and parish.

About that time inaccurate information about doctrines from the Second Vatican Council came out. I remember sitting on the church steps talking to a school friend who told me she had heard we didn't need to go to individual confession to a priest anymore, that just confessing in church to God was enough. Big mistake! Jesus gave to Peter and His Apostles the authority, indeed the mandate, to hear confessions in His name saying "Whose sins you shall forgive they are forgiven; whose sins you shall retain they are retained." Though Mom and Dad invested 4 years for me to attend a wonderful Catholic high school in the city, Cor Jesu Academy, I did not forget that statement and the damage played out in my adult amoral life.

Years later, while a forester in Sullivan, I became irritated about something and used that as an excuse to quit going to Mass. More and more I was losing contact with a religion I had barely begun to become familiar with. I can only be very grateful that God has perfect memory and did not forget me, His favorite child. (We are each His favorite child!)

The forest was my religion and communication with my God. And I had a great love and respect for the trees, His precious gift. I wonder if that had something to do with why I tried to stop the abuse at Bluffwoods by alleged devil worshipers. The awful images painted on the bathroom walls were appalling. Never have I seen such disgusting things painted on bathroom walls. How could this exist on our state land so close to the city of St. Joseph?

Though I felt uneasy going through the picnic grounds, I was probably too naive to be afraid. St. Michael the Archangel must have been looking out for me. If I knew then what I know now, I would have been more afraid. I couldn't understand why these horrible things could happen in a city named for that gentle saint and guardian of the child Jesus, St. Joseph. Being demoted and moving back to Franklin County outside of St. Louis made no difference in my worship practices, or rather lack thereof. When my position in forestry fell apart I plunged into serious depression. Still I did not find solace, or blame, in my religion, it was just there.

In 1994 I moved back to the Webster Groves area of St. Louis, getting ever closer to where I grew up. I later advertised for a roommate to share my 2-bedroom apartment and met Pat who took me to the Charismatic Mass held in Holy Redeemer Church. I had been going to church only occasionally, I was not a good Catholic. It still took a month later before I returned to the Charismatic Mass. I had what people call a conversion, or being born again. I returned, joyfully, to the sacraments. The joy, the peace, the love, the forgiveness is beyond all understanding. I owe my life to my friend who almost had to drag me to church that first Saturday night. From that day on my life changed forever.

I could not go to church often enough for Mass, retreats, spiritual direction, rosaries or any reason at all to be close to Him. Confession, what we now call Reconciliation, and forgiveness are so important.

When I stopped Reconciliation and the Eucharist, I lost life. But Jesus never let go.

Thank you to Sister Marie, and Janie and Judy. I could not make it without The Prayer of Command they shared with me. And thank you Sister Charlotte and the members of the healing and deliverance teams I prayed with and shared my gifts with.

It has been wonderful, Christ is very generous with His gifts. I even have had a small intercessory prayer group in my home. Marian and Joseph and Christine and others have been very helpful. I take great pleasure in interfering with the evil one's plans, and God has rewarded me. The gifts of joy and peace have come through extraordinary personal revelation, so much that I could fill volumes, and so little that I thirst for much more. And this is available to each of us. His forgiveness is beyond all understanding, and the New Wine! Wow! Nobody throws a party like Jesus!

I want to thank the friends I have made in the church. In the Charismatic Renewal I found angels. Christine has driven my accessible van to the Charismatic Mass on Saturday nights for 3 years. These masses and the music and praying, and the blessed priests, and mostly the Eucharist, are so wonderful.

And my parish, St. Michael the Archangel, has provided great friends. Trish and her husband Jim rescued me last winter when my furnace shut down, and consoled me when I fell apart. Thank you, Myco, who also seems to show up when I crash and burn with Jesus, and Lily who brings me homemade meals and has brought a group to dedicate my home to His Sacred Heart. And my neighbor visits and brings me food. And thank you for our pastor who comes and brings me Jesus and Reconciliation, and the anointing of the sick when I just can't go on anymore. And thank you to Jane, my very good friend in the Charismatic Renewal, who is a member of my parish, who brings Jesus to me daily.

And how many angels will He send me tomorrow? Thank you

PART 5

Emotions

"The Only Thing We Have to Fear Is Fear Itself"
PRESIDENT FR ANKLIN ROOSEVELT
1st inaugural address, March 4, 1933

CHAPTER 25

Dealing With Fear

IT IS SAID PREDATORY ANIMALS can smell fear and sense when to go in for the kill. I thought that an exaggeration, but it isn't, it stinks!

As an arborist, I attended what conferences I could afford and when I had vacation time available. I registered for the International Society of Arboriculture [ISA] annual conference at Hilton Head Island, South Carolina. But the m.s. was becoming very unmanageable. I was scared, and almost didn't go. But at the last moment I decided to try to make it. What did I have to lose? This is the story of my drive, alone of course.

It was 1995, over 10 years after I had been diagnosed with multiple sclerosis. It was 5 years since I had been demoted out of forestry, and 1½ years after being promoted into urban forestry. I wanted to drive to Hilton Head for the ISA Conference and Tree Climbing Competition. The M.S. was causing my walking to be more erratic with weaving and fatigue. I met with a new neurology and during a 15-minute meeting, this neurologist advised me to immediately get on a particular medicine because the M.S. could take a turn for the worse at any time leaving me permanently crippled. But this medicine was for relapsing remitting not chronic progressive.

Though having misgivings, I was committed to the trip. I left in 100 degree heat and the heat stayed with me from St. Louis for two days and one very hot night camping in Illinois. Fear stayed with me; I constantly considered turning around if I could even make it back. I noted every hospital and every doctor sign along the way, ready to check into a hospital at any moment. I even called my regular doctor, and his nurse assured me things would work out. I kept taking one mile, one town, at a time, not knowing if I would make the next mile. In route, I camped out in Illinois because camping is what I do even in 100 degrees heat. Motels are so sterile and impersonal.

I couldn't help but notice a strange odor in the car despite the air conditioning. It wouldn't go away, it didn't smell like anything mechanical, but it was sickening. My fears were growing. The second day I was coming to the halfway mark, where I would have to turn south through the Tennessee mountains.

I knew I couldn't handle the traffic through Gatlinburg going over the mountains, and I just couldn't go any farther east. It was now or never. I headed south through a pass I noted on the road map, feeling absolutely rotten, and the smell was over-powering. It did not seem to be affecting my driving, so I went on, thinking I could turn around, but not knowing what was ahead. The country was getting more remote which was more scary, but far more enjoyable. The road was gaining in elevation. I felt a little better. The road went higher still and the air was cooler. I felt less anxious, not much but anything was better than the last day and a half in the hot, flat lands.

I passed a large Corps of Engineers lake project. There were a few trees blooming purple along the road and parking areas and I just had to check. They were paulownia. Though a nuisance species in many areas they were a welcome site. The blooms were pretty and I sort of felt that I was among friends. I stayed awhile, ate a little, and got back in the car. Although the car was still rank, it seemed better, I traveled on. The next hour the road going up was steeper and really winding.

I stopped again at an overlook, the road was really winding and climbing steadily. You would think I would be fearful, but I drove a lot of narrow, winding roads as a forester, and I was surrounded by woods, I felt home again. I was home. Surrounded by trees in the cooler air, I was home and it was wonderful.

There was a primitive Forest Service campground just over the crest of the hill. I put up a tent for changing, but I slept out in the open. The ground was covered with pine needles. Tulip poplars, oaks, white pines, maples and hemlocks towered over me. The forest smell was wonderful, even the car smelled fresh and clean. I knew what the odor had been, and I knew it was gone. I had reeked of fear, and I lost it in the forest. I didn't light a campfire, because I didn't want to ruin the scenery and woods smell with the light. I slept deeper than I had in so long. Since I lost forestry, I had not spent a great deal of time in the woods. I miss the woods. The poet Robert Frost understood when he wrote "The woods are lovely, dark and deep..."

So there I was, sitting on my couch in an apartment in the city working on my memoirs. I wrote these words years ago; then I rewrote them multiple times. It was very healing to spill out my emotions into the many pages. I had forgotten the seriousness of my condition at that time; the emotions were fresher in my mind when I originally wrote this script:

"For two days I lived in fear. My stomach churned as if held by a violent stomach flu. My defecation came in spurts and gushes that would make a cow envious. Hot flashes seared through my body, challenging the car's air conditioning and making motivation with the m.s. all but impossible. Numbness from the m.s. galloped up my body from my lower legs and often stretched into my arms and hands so that I feared I could not drive and stopped to let the feeling pass, to go on again. Spasms gripped my groin on the right side and knocked my legs out from under me so I found myself balanced precariously until the spasms passed."

The rest of the trip to the meeting, the International Society of Arboriculture annual meeting, was good, though camping at night on Hilton Head was hot, 100 degrees, and the sand fleas were moving in as I was moving out. On the way home I took another route and camped again in the mountains; it was beautiful. Took another route through Southern Illinois also, and made it safely home.

Fear was an evil emotion, it drained my energy and haunted me for decades. Fear of losing my cherished career for which I had given up so much, including pride and self-respect, haunted me. On December 25, 1991, I started reclaiming my life. I declared my independence from fear. I actually wrote the director of my employer begging him to fire me. I stated I didn't have the guts to quit; getting insurance for someone with m.s. is impossible.

I didn't quite understand at the time, but I wrote the letter because I was tired of living with fear. After that I was quite brazen about my attitude, to anyone who would listen. Every time I heard myself state my feelings to others in the agency, I became stronger. I had been paralyzed with fear about losing my insurance. I had already lost my career.

After 23 full years I retired with long-term disability, officially 12/1/02. I am now, 2012, retired 10 years. I can't worry about tomorrow; it doesn't matter, it's coming anyway. I can only take one day at a time. I have turned my worries over to Jesus, He is my strength and support. Being a weak human I tend to take the fear back. Things can get really, really bad, but tomorrow is another day. A fear that tears us down and haunts us is not of God. The apostles dealt with fear, but not always very well, all but John abandoned Jesus as He died on the Cross for us. Jesus forgave them their weakness and promised to send the Paraclete to strengthen them. And He did. We can do all things with God who strengthens us.

"Success is not measured by what a man accomplishes, but by the opposition he has overcome and the courage with which he maintained the struggle against overwhelming odds".
ORISON SWETT MARSDEN

CHAPTER 26

Dealing With Depression

I'VE BEEN THERE, AND I don't ever want to go back. I believe I know the warning signs, and by God, I know how to fight it. When my career fell apart I started to cry, I gave in to crying. It was an escape, allowing me to waste time feeling sorry for myself rather than deal with the problem and come up with solutions. It was my way of running away.

I tried fighting the awful things said about me and the probation. But I didn't know how., and I probably believed them that I was a terrible employee and deserved the terrible things happening, just as I believed I did something terrible to deserve the M.S. Everything was all my fault.

Well, it ain't.

I can't go back and fix the past. My days of walking in the woods are over, but life goes on. In many ways it is better. I came back to my church and have known joy beyond all understanding, despite the M.S. Depression is not of God.

Oh, I still get depressed dealing with this disease. It's understandable and I have to allow myself some time for grieving., a few minutes to feel sorry for myself, and then back to reality. If it goes on, then I have a prayer that quickly brings me peace. It's pretty obvious things are working, for I haven't shed a tear over the final rewriting of this book.. Believe me I shed plenty for the two decades I have been writing this book. Each rewrite things softened and the anger and the tears decreased.

And I have learned from the trees in so many ways. After trees seal a wound with hard, callous tissue they continue to grow, covering even the callous tissue leaving only a visible knot. In time even that may cover. Wounds to the mind and heart do not heal so much as with time they seal. But before they can safely seal, forgiveness must prevail. If not, they can fester inside, and come back to the surface like hidden decay in a tree.

I have memorized this prayer and it has always brought me peace, against all odds.

A PRAYER OF COMMAND

In the name of Jesus Christ, and by the power of His cross and blood, I bind any evil spirits, forces, or powers of earth, air, fire, or water, of the nether world, and the satanic forces of nature. By the sword of the Spirit, and by the authority given to me by Jesus Christ, I break any curses, hexes, or spells, and send them back to where they came from. I plead the protection of the shed blood of Jesus Christ on my....., and command that any departing spirits leave quietly, without causing any disturbance, and go straight to Jesus Christ for Him to deal with them as He sees fit.

AUTHOR UNKNOWN

"A tree takes a long time to grow, and wounds take a long time to heal. But we must begin."
WILLIAM JEFFERSON CLINTON, April 23, 1995
Oklahoma Bombing Memorial Prayer Service
Address, Oklahoma City OK

CHAPTER 27

Dealing With Emotions

PITY

A GOOD FRIEND GAVE ME A picture of a baby on a pot and advised me to "get off the pity pot." Well, I am still trying with God's help, and I keep the pity pot nearby for emergencies. Self pity is very self destructive. It is an evil that tears you up inside. We don't need others to feel sorry for us either, they have their own problems. We do not need to feel sorry for others, that makes us co-dependents.

We probably start feeling sorry for ourselves as children, but eventually we have to grow up. Lingering over a problem makes the problem grow and our spirits wither. We must strengthen our own self worth, so that we are not fragile. Self-help books may help some, but a better way can be to tell others how wonderful they are. People need to be needed, let people help you without taking advantage of them. Help other people without letting them take advantage of you. Treat others with respect.

Many, because they are going through a bad time, are unable to return the favor. Trust the Lord to return multiple blessings. Maybe someday they will soften. Guard yourself as necessary without putting up walls. Some relationships can be toxic to you. Find groups that work for you. Find groups that will say good things to you. Find groups that will be honest, but tactful; groups that will help you grow. And then let your subconscious soak it in. And get off the pity pot.

GRIEF

Something inside me died that day in '89, I lost hope. When something bad happens it takes time to recover. But it helps to see the good that comes out of bad. I had to say goodbye to a way of life. I sold my farm. No longer will I see those proud wiry hens strut before my door leading a dozen or so chicks. No longer will my horse peer in through the window to watch the activities. No longer will my dog chase away intruders. It wasn't just the loss of a career and a way of life, I lost hope. I told myself I did not care, but I cared too much.

There are important things in life. The job and the health insurance rated very high, high enough to stay where I was not wanted. Retirement with the disability came when I had enough. If I had made adjustments such as with a scooter and conversion van I could have worked longer, but I just didn't think of it. And my employer was happy to finally retire me. I don't miss the job, but I miss the forest. I volunteered at the Missouri Botanical Garden Plant Doctor desk after retiring, and did quarterly newsletters, *The Urban Tree*. I hope to continue doing programs, I have a projector-computer and 20 cd's full of tree pictures, but no longer driving complicates things. Maybe I'll write, but energy is limited.

I don't think about my past life. Grief does not really heal, it just seals, like a wound on a tree. I have learned many lessons about survival from trees, let me have the heart of a healthy tree with strong roots. Let me cling to life regardless of how nature, man and disease challenge me. Trees don't grieve loss, they just keep growing as long as they can.

ANGER

Yes I was angry. I was angry at my own body, it goes its own direction. I was tired of bouncing off walls, of falling down, now I'm tired of the scooter. I am tired of bladder and bowel dysfunction. The scooter is a real benefit, but not without its challenges. I miss driving.

I was angry that my brother Richard died and left such a mess for me to clean up. I was angry and hurt that my other older brother made such negative comments about Rich's country home. He was zero help to me on the estate settlement and made things difficult from a distance, ask my attorney. Thank God because the settlement was in a neighboring state I met an attorney, Randy, who has been a wonderful help to me over several years, and I consider a special friend. Also thank you Peggy, Mom's neighbor who spent at least two long, hard days with me.

I was angry that my family left me alone to help my mother. I was angry that my father died, he wasn't ready at 92, but things happen. I was angry that my mother died and left me physically alone, but not spiritually.

I am angry that the M.S. keeps making me so sick and tired. And yes I was angry at God for letting this happen to me, and I have told God. Yet I love God so much, and depend on Him for everything. Maybe that is why I can get angry with Him. I tried to tell my dead brother how hurt I was for his not being here and holding me in his arms and protecting me as a big brother should do for his little sister.

I doubt that in recent history there ever lived a people who suffered so much loss as the American Indian, our Native Americans. They lost it all, their medicines, their lodges, their hunting grounds, their food, their families, their health, their way of life, their history. Their bodies were mutilated, their spirits twisted with insults. Were it not for their children they would probably have fought to the death and extinction.

Sometimes it helps to get angry, sometimes it helps to cry. Knowing when to put a halt on anger and other negative emotions is very important for survival and growth. Looking back doesn't work; you must look forward. Anger can release a lot of pent up energy, but then so can exercise, and that is a more positive use of energy.

"Anger is an invitation to change.
Forgiveness is the answer."
CHARLOTTE E. SCHNEIDER

*"Seek not to understand that you may believe,
but believe that you may understand."*
SAINT AUGUSTINE

CHAPTER 28

Embracing Trust

I DON'T UNDERSTAND THE WEATHER IN Missouri. It can tumble 50 degrees in a few hours, and warm again as quickly. Summers will be hot and humid, most of the time, when it is not cold and rainy. Fall will see the temperatures drop as well as the leaves of deciduous trees, generally with brilliant color.Winter will be cold, with freezing rain and maybe snow, then spring will bring the blossoms of flowers and flowering trees, unless they were hit by a late frost. These things we can trust.

The sun will rise tomorrow, even if clouds hide it from us. Rain will fall, somewhere. And somewhere in the woods an oak acorn will sprout and a new tree will begin to grow and an old tree will die. We need to learn early in life how to discern what can be trusted and what cannot. Do not put blind trust in an organization of people, people make mistakes.

When 28 I returned to college. I trusted that if I studied hard and worked hard I could develop a career in forestry. I graduated from college with honors. I started working for Parks and Recreation in Little Rock, Arkansas. Though temporary I was promoted into a permanent position. I trusted the people I worked with and they trusted me.

Then I was offered a forestry position in my home state. I trusted things would go as in Little Rock, but I was wrong. After ten years of silence, I learned what they thought of me. And I let my world fall apart. I know I was a good forester, but I failed to communicate that to the powers that be. As things progressed with the m.s., I had hoped I could adjust my work day to my disability, but it was not acceptable. I never wanted anyone to take care of me, but I was naive enough to not consider they would take the opportunity of my transfer to get rid of me, I should have known.

I wanted to quit and move on, but when I mentioned M.S. to prospective employers, they seemed to back off. Sure I could have lied, but what a way to start a new job carrying this deep dark secret until it became obvious. No thanks. So I held on despite losing forestry. It was humiliating working out of a storage room without a desk or phone or window or other amenities after working in the woods. My every move seemed to be watched.

When you get to that point, you acquire a certain freedom. When you don't care whether you live or die, then you don't particularly care whether you get fired. Though my attitude was at an all time low, my work ethic was deep and I continued to work hard. But I freely proclaimed my bad attitude. They did not fire me, and after 3½ years the district forester presented a proposal to me that would put me back into forestry--urban forestry. Could I trust them? Could they trust me?

Did I jump at the chance? You bet. It was a chance to be a forester again, and learn something new. Though I was restricted mostly to the desk and phone most days, every day was a new learning experience. I was able to do forestry programs and became active with the local arborist associations. I became the department's first Certified Arborist and trained arborists for a few years.

My supervisor was knowledgeable and treated me decent. He tried to get me out, but afternoon sun destroyed my stamina. He accepted my challenges even better than I did, but my health continued to deteriorate. And when I retired with the disability, 9 years later, they threw a party for me and my friends at the Arboretum in Grey Summit. It was wonderful. No one from the headquarters office showed up.

I take one day at a time expecting nothing for the future, and not looking back to the past, except to write this book. Being retired, I have worn out several scooters and a conversion van. I had been volunteering weekly at the Missouri Botanical Garden as a Plant Doctor and even became a Master Gardener, though my knowledge of flowers is truly marginal. I recognize the very important role the community of plants plays in the environment. And the volunteers I worked with are very remarkable, knowledgeable, dedicated people.

So what should we trust? Trust is marginal in this technological world where a new computer is obsolete before it is even unpacked. Companies downsize and cast employees away as dust in the wind. Before the recession, many employees jumped from company to company for more money and more amenities, without developing loyalty to an organization.

I do trust. I trust God. He doesn't promise riches and wealth. He doesn't promise a life without pain. He does promise that He loves us. On that we can depend. He promises to give us the strength to survive the bad times as well as the good times. He made the sun and the moon, the mountains and valleys formed in response to His rain. The plants and animals respond to the seasons following the cycles in the turning of the earth. The trees respond to His sun and wind and rain. He made all things good. And I love Him, and I trust Him.

> *"Trust the past to the mercy of God, the present to*
> *His love, the future to His providence."*
> SAINT AUGUSTINE

Received this on a greeting card from Jim Brewer, to whom I am eternally grateful for helping me find my way to forestry

"You can't believe the joy!"
Heard on Covenant Network–St. Louis Catholic radio.
A young seminarian was dying but in excruciating pain.
Pope John Paul II gave special permission to ordain him.
Told by Father John Corapi

CHAPTER 29

Joy to the World

BELIEVE IT! I HAVE HAD to give up <u>total</u> control of my life to God. And the joy that has come with that is beyond measure. Though I am far from worthy, I have taken Jesus as my spouse and so much more. He is everything to me. God is my mother, my father, my children, my grandparents, my nieces and nephews, my everything. Nothing else matters but to do His will. And in doing so, I receive joy and peace beyond all understanding.

Oh don't get me wrong, I am no saint! There was a poster of God the Father as portrayed in the Sistine Chapel outside my bathroom in my apartment I was known to throw my shoe at in frustration. He hears exactly what I think of this disease in words I will only describe here as colorful, and usually beyond the top of my voice into a blood-curdling scream. This disease comes straight from hell, yes there is a hell. And this is as much as I can bear of it To do something to seriously incur the wrath of God and then die, is really scary. I could have to deal with this forever. Aughhhhhh! Enough of that.

Better the joy. Other people who pray in tongues know the freedom and peace and happiness that comes with that gift. Likely other people who have experienced the gift of Holy Laughter from the Holy Spirit, know what I am trying to express here. The gifts of knowledge and understanding that have expressed themselves in me at times have given me to see and appreciate deeper the richness of my faith. This Catholic faith is far beyond all measure of understanding. It has survived 2000 years filled with saints who have suffered unbearable torture, and still the faith goes on today. It survived the foibles and sinful practices of leaders in the hierarchy. It has survived the schisms of past centuries, and will survive those of our own day, including the so-called women's lib movement and all its unholy and deadly machinations. This Holy Church is God driven, and He is liberating.

I have been there in the dead zone. I was liberated enough as a single woman to get a tubal ligation for obvious reasons. Bet that was a shock medically to my system, confusing my hormones. I have imbibed enough scotch and martinis, stirred not shaken, to float a boat. Never did drugs, thank God, they just didn't appeal to me. And one thing I can tell you for certain: No body throws a party like Jesus. The ecstasy of His new wine is without measure. He freed women when He walked on the earth, like when He talked to the woman at the well, and when He wrote on the ground distracting a stoning. Remember He was 9 months in Mary's womb, and suckled at her breast. Without sinning, He broke many old Jewish laws and laid the foundation for our religion, a religion of repentance, where we can be freed of the burden of our sins through confession to His priests.

Don't believe me? Read the early church Fathers, with an open mind and heart. Read Saint Francis of Assisi, Saint Augustine, Saint Benedict, Saints Theresa and other saints and Doctors of His Church. And don't be surprised what you learn, but always discern. Know that where there is good, there can also be found evil. Jesus paid the price for our sins, He bore our sins in the marks of the lash, and He took them to The Father when He hung on the cross, and then He declared "It is finished." Study Him, pray to Him, talk to Him...He is the best friend you will ever have.

AFTERWORD:.

I CURRENTLY, SEPTEMBER 2012, REQUIRE 24-7 care, but I have lovely care-givers. Renee Quackenbush is my personal assistant and primary care-giver. She is bound and determined to make me healthy and independent again. Noni fruit is her primary effective health builder, however through research she is exploring with me many alternatives. And she is a strong supporter of chia seeds and other anti-oxidants and nutrition builders. I am a strong advocate of Reliv and exercise; however, Renee is making me eat also. Gotta watch my weight.

Though the M.S. has abused my body, it has not reduced my desire to keep tree communities in the forefront of people's consideration. My home and surrounding 6750 sq. ft. I have turned into an arboretum studying different trees, shrubs and plants dealing with competition and weather. About them I blog regularly with text and pictures as health permits. I also reminisce about my days in the forest. You can find my blogs through Google under Our Little Urban Arboretum or Female Forester Forever. Renee has taken me once again to meetings of the Saint Louis Arborist Association. I will probably lose my status as a Certified Arborist unless my blogging can save me which is sad.

Tomorrow?

CONCLUSION

About the Author

A TRADITIONAL LIFE TURNED UPSIDE DOWN on a wing and a prayer. Who would have thought a city slicker secretary could find peace cruising timber, and pride helping landowners understand their forest resource. Disappearing into the woods for hours became as natural as walking to the corner ice cream store.

But the lessons learned from trees and from making a major change in life go way beyond anything taught in schools. Forestry worked magic in my life. Though probably, I came by a search for adventure and willingness to take risks from my parents who emigrated from Germany almost a century ago. They met in Saint Louis, married, and raised 3 children. I was the youngest, and the only girl. Having their only girl run off to the woods may have been hard to understand, but forestry was esteemed in Europe, and that helped. My mother's father would go to the Black Forest in Germany to collect mushrooms.

Adjusting to primary progressive multiple sclerosis, and to rejection and loss of this hard won career, took a lot out of me. But I survived deep depression, and I live to tell you how. There is always the ability to "turn over a new leaf".

Worked 3 years for the Wood Products Lab, University of Missouri School of Forestry Work Study program

Past member & Vice President of *Xi Sigma Pi*, honorary forestry fraternity

Graduated *cum laude* with a Bachelor of Science in Forest Management

Worked 1 year for the Little Rock Parks & Recreation as a Planner

Charlotte Schneider

I was one of the first 10 women employed by state governments to serve
private landowners.

As a Forester serving private forest landowners and fighting forest fires,
I worked 10 years on the Meramec Forest District in Missouri

American Tree Farm System award recipient

Worked 2 years as a Forester on the Saint Joseph Forest District

Worked 3 months on the Angeles National Forest District as a Fire
Fighter

Worked 9 years on the Saint Louis Forest District as an Urban
Forester

Certified Arborist 1988 to date

Taught & Administered Certified Arborist Exams 4 years

Have an Honorary Lifetime Membership in the Midwestern Chapter,
International Society of Arboriculture, and The Saint Louis
Arborist Association

Volunteered 9 years for the Missouri Botanical Garden as a Plant Doctor
and Master Gardener

35 total years as a Forester